THE TRIUMPHANT JUAN RANA:
A GAY ACTOR OF THE SPANISH GOLDEN AGE

PETER E. THOMPSON

The Triumphant Juan Rana:

A Gay Actor of the Spanish Golden Age

UNIVERSITY OF TORONTO PRESS
Toronto Buffalo London

ISBN-13: 978-0-8020-8969-4
ISBN-10: 0-8020-8969-0

Printed on acid-free paper

Library and Archives Canada Cataloguing in Publication

Thompson, Peter E.
  The triumphant Juan Rana : a gay actor of the Spanish golden age / Peter E.
Thompson.

  (University of Toronto romance series)
  Includes bibliographical references and index.
  ISBN-13: 978-0-8020-8969-4
  ISBN-10: 0-8020-8969-0

  1. Rana, Juan.   2. Actors – Spain – Biography.   3. Gay actors –
  Spain – Biography.
  I. Title.   II. Series.

  PN2788.R36T46 2006   792.02'8'092   C2006-900346-7

University of Toronto Press acknowledges the financial assistance to
its publishing program of the Canada Council for the Arts and the
Ontario Arts Council.

This book has been published with the help of a grant from the
Canadian Federation for the Humanities and Social Sciences, through
the Aid to Scholarly Publications Programme, using funds provided by
the Social Sciences and Humanities Research Council of Canada.

University of Toronto Press acknowledges the financial support for
its publishing activities of the Government of Canada through the
Book Publishing Industry Development Program (BPIDP).

For the Love and Joy of Chata and Pepe

Contents

Acknowledgments

I wish to express my gratitude to the Department of Spanish, Italian and Portuguese and the College of the Liberal Arts of Penn State for their support during the initial stages of the writing of this book. I am exceedingly grateful to Dr Margaret Lyday for her editorial, moral, and emotional support during this period. I am especially indebted to Dr Frederick de Armas and Dr Martha Halsey, with whom I have had the honour and pleasure to study and work. Notably, it was Dr de Armas who suggested I work on Juan Rana.

Many friends have been tremendously important during the various phases of the book's writing. Dr Jennifer Zachman and Anne Scott were my Penn State partners in crime. Dr Donna Rogers has also been there since the Penn State days giving much academic, moral, and good-humoured support. Dr Jackie Campbell has kept me going with many chats and original cards. Dr Stephanie Inglis and Peyton Chisholm have always managed to bolster the morale. Shirley Nunn has been there during the cloudy Gananoque days with her kind friendship and words of wisdom. The individually unique and unequalled camaraderie of Juan Irigoyen, Carlos Zamora, Concha Alarcón, Elena and Sergio Moline, Jeff Munro, and Ramón Cuenca has enhanced my life and ultimately, aided in the writing of this book. And of course, my long friendship with José María López-Saiz has been greatly influential in my life and career choice.

Editorially, Curtis Fahey and Stephanie Stone's know-how were much appreciated. As well, my graduate assistant, Marla Arbach, has been indispensable in the final months of the editing process. Her keen eye for detail has been a godsend and crucial in the difficult task of translating the original texts. The staff of the University of Toronto Press have of course been pivotal in this endeavour, especially Jill McConkey, Barbara Porter, and Miriam Skey.

I am also grateful to the Real Academia Española for permission to reproduce the extraordinary Juan Rana portrait from their collection. I thank Elvira Fernández del Pozo for her gracious assistance in this matter.

I am especially indebted to the incredible friendship and generosity of Gloria Di Folco and Dr Donato Santeramo. Donato's culinary savoir faire, judicious encouragement, and editorial expertise were especially appreciated.

Finally, I am very grateful for the family support I have received from Caterina, David, Gillian, and Ian Lake-Thompson.

THE TRIUMPHANT JUAN RANA:
A GAY ACTOR OF THE SPANISH GOLDEN AGE

1 What's in a Name?[1]

Juan Rana's long and successful acting career spanned the period from 1617 to 1672, one of the most important periods in Spanish history and theatre. He was the star of the Spanish baroque *entremés*, or theatrical interlude and a major drawing card – much like the *entremés* itself – that ensured the financial success of the theatre production as a whole. This actor's popularity and *fama* was not limited to the rowdy *mosqueteros* (groundling spectators)[2] standing in front of the stage; he was also greatly esteemed and even protected by the powerful noble class and the monarchy. Maria Luisa Lobato states that '[l]a vida y el trabajo actoral de Cosme Pérez, alias Juan Rana, estuvo vinculada a la Casa Real y concretamente a la Casa de la Reina, y la llegada de Mariana de Austria a la Corte no hizo más que aumentar esta relación y aprecio' (80) (the life and theatrical work of Cosme Pérez, alias Juan Rana, was linked to the royal house and concretely to the house of the queen, and the arrival at court of Mariana of Austria did nothing but increase this relationship and esteem).[3] Significantly, the later part of the actor's life embodies

> uno de los aspectos más intensos de la historia del teatro español áureo, para reivindicar la presencia de un grupo de actores cerca de la familia real, con especial insistencia Juan Rana, de quien Felipe IV dejó testimonios de primera mano, que prueban el favor de que gozó por parte del penúltimo de los Austrias y de su familia. (111)

one of the most intense aspects of the history of Spanish Golden Age theatre, which bears witness to the presence of a group of actors close to the royal family, especially Juan Rana, of whom Felipe IV left first-hand accounts, which prove the favour he enjoyed at the hands of the second-last head of the house of Austria and his family.

Not surprisingly, many of his later performances were command performances at the newly expanded and renovated theatre of the Retiro palace, more evidence of the magnitude of his status as an actor.

One such royal command performance was his last – *El triunfo de Juan Rana* (1670).[4] This laudatory *entremés*, in which Juan Rana plays himself, was especially created for the actor by Pedro Calderón de la Barca and is included in one of Calderón's last plays, *Fieras afemina amor* (Wilson 17). It is precisely in this last *entremés* that Calderón crowns Juan Rana *el máximo gracioso* or the greatest buffoon of his time (115). The *entremés* in its entirety is a public celebration of Juan Rana's great talent and his long and successful career as an actor. As Calderón was the most important and influential playwright of his time, his celebratory *entremés* bears witness to the public and professional *fama* and acclaim that Juan Rana enjoyed during his lifetime. Many of the best playwrights of the period also wrote specifically for Juan Rana. Over fifty Juan Rana specific *entremeses* have been documented and an uncanny number of these contain his name as part of the title (Serralta 91–2; Cotarelo y Mori clxiii). Many of those who wrote specifically for him were nobles directly linked to the royal court. Fortunately, Juan Rana's courtly connections would be his saving grace. In one critical brush with the law, Juan Rana was spared from an untimely end due to the intervention of those in high places.

Emilio Cotarelo y Mori's general introduction to his monumental *Colección de entremeses, loas, bailes, jácaras y mojigangas desde fines del siglo XVI a mediados del XVIII* (1911) devotes seven pages to Juan Rana's life and career (clvii–clxiii) while all other actors receive a mere mention. The importance that this revered early twentieth-century *entremesil* critic gives to Juan Rana is a testimony to his grand legacy. From the detailed biographical material included in this introductory study we learn that Juan Rana was born at the end of the sixteenth century and died in 1672. While christened Cosme Pérez, his stage name Juan Rana became so famous that he is said to have signed documents under it. In other words, the actor gave life not only to a persona but also to a new personal identity.

Evangelina Rodríguez documents the historical legacy of Juan Rana and his created mask, or persona, explaining that

> la única máscara, el único personaje-mito ... del que podríamos aducir y reconstruir una sucinta genealogía, se levanta, precisamente, desde el denso microcosmos del entremés. Hablamos, claro, del entrañable y estrafalario 'Juan Rana.' El estudio de la actividad histriónica en España durante el

Siglo de Oro ... da mayor margen de seguridad a la hipótesis de que el personaje de 'Juan Rana,' como el Arlequín de la *commedia dell'arte*, fue una mascara creada posiblemente a partir de las habilidades técnicas y de la composición corporal de un actor, en este caso Cosme Pérez, pero cuya instauración como mito hubo de realizarse por la herencia efectiva de dicho tipo de un actor a otro, tal vez de una generación a otra. (566)

the only mask, the only character-myth ... for which we can allege and reconstruct a succint genealogy, crops up precisely within the dense microcosm of the *entremés*. We are speaking, obviously, of the dearly loved and eccentric 'Juan Rana.' The study of histrionic activity in Spain during the Golden Age ... gives more certainty to the hypothesis that the character of 'Juan Rana,' like Harlequin in the Commedia dell'Arte, was a mask based possibly on the technical abilities and the physical features of an actor, in this case Cosme Pérez, but whose founding as a myth must have effectively been made possible by the passing down of said character type from one actor to another, perhaps from one generation to another.

Considering that the Juan Rana persona obtained a mythical status similar to that of the Italian Harlequin and that his legacy was kept alive by generations of actors and symbolic references to him, the man himself must surely have been extremely entertaining and spectacular.[5]

In general terms, Juan Rana's success was based on a stereotheatrical persona. The audience of this period was well accustomed to this persona and expected to see and experience a well-established and defined mode of histrionic behaviour as Rodríguez has shown (566). Juan Rana, as is to be expected of a *gracioso* (buffoon), represented the weak, feeble-minded, and laughable *chivo expiatorio*. He also personified the unworldly country bumpkin, an *entremesil* topos that easily delighted the urban theatre audience. Apart from his rustic attire and *gestus*, Juan Rana's histrionic social position of inferiority was verbally portrayed through his *sayagués* mode of speaking.[6] Juan Rana misinterpreted and misused language, as would the bumbling and gullible buffoon that he played. While it cannot be denied that the great success of this actor was based on his superior histrionic abilities, there exists, nevertheless, a far-reaching component of Juan Rana's life that imparted a particular meaning and reading to his stage appearances and greatly contributed to his fame. Juan Rana was arrested for the *pecado nefando* in 1636, an event that could have ended tragically considering his crime and the official punishment for it.

In the early modern era the term *pecado nefando* referred to all *contra naturam* sexual activity. Jonathan Goldberg explains that the concept of natural order in seventeenth-century Europe, as understood by the church and, hence, by law and society, meant procreative sex practised within the bounds of holy matrimony (19). This strict definition of natural sexual activity excluded any act *extra vas naturale*, be it masturbation, fellatio, anal sex, or bestiality. Any aberrant sexual activity was seen to be *contra naturam* and hence connected to 'heterodoxies of all sorts: sorcery, religious heresy, treason' (Smith 11). Based on the cruel and extreme punishments described in the Old Testament, punishment for the *pecado nefando* included castration, burning at the stake, the *galeras,* appropriation of goods and property, and banishment (Pérez Escohotado 176). While the actual punishment for the *pecado nefando* varied according to the particulars of each case and the period in which the transgression took place, in most instances the individual paid a high price for his *contra naturam* pleasure.

Rafael Carrasco, in his historical account of the Inquisition and sexual repression in Valencia and on the Iberian Peninsula from the sixteenth to the eighteenth century, paints a grim portrait of homosexual practice and its punishment. Through a detailed analysis of inquisitional and other legal documents, this critic shows the universal aberrance and intolerance for any homosexual act or mere show of affection between two men. What emerges from his account is a sordid picture of conspiratorial informants among the masses, an abusive noble and ecclesiastical class taking full advantage of their powerless and youthful underlings, and a general atmosphere of marginalized licentious, physical, and aggressive coupling void of compassion and affection. Carrasco recognizes the existence of 'un verdadero *ghetto* homosexual superpoblado donde se cruzan soldados, artesanos, burócratas y hasta el verdurgo' (66) (a veritable overpopulated homosexual ghetto where soldiers, artisans, bureaucrats, and even executioners rub shoulders) but at the same time states that this marginalized space does by no means constitute a homosexual community. As such, the repressive and generalized fear caused by the Inquisition and religious beliefs and the great differences of class and power were hostile to any nurturing homosexual relationship.[7]

Antonio Rodríguez Villa's *La corte y monarquía de España en los años de 1636 y 1637* (1886) documents Juan Rana's arrest and at the same time assumes a moral stance on the empire's deplorable legal and social state of affairs:

En cuanto al negocio de los que están presos por el pecado nefando, no se usa del rigor que se esperaba, o sea esto porque el ruido ha sido mayor que las nueces, o sea que verdaderamente el poder y el dinero alcanzan lo que quieran. A Don Nicolás, el paje del Conde de Castrillo, vemos que anda por la calle, y a Juan Rana, famoso representante, han soltado, y no vemos quemar á ninguno de cuantos presos hay. (68)

As regards the business of those who are imprisoned for the *pecado nefando*, punishment is not as severe as one would hope, either because the whole thing was much ado about nothing, or because power and money really get what they want. We see that Don Nicolás, the Count of Castrillo's page, is out on the street, and that Juan Rana, the famous actor, has been released, and not many prisoners are being burned.

Apart from the mention of Juan Rana and his accomplice, the author, quite obviously, laments the lack of severity shown to those accused of the nefarious sin and, in doing so, hints at what he perceives as a weakening in moral and social standards. Carrasco has shown that during the period of Juan Rana's arrest repression of homosexuals was indeed decreasing (73). This fact combined with the actor's close relationship with the noble class and the reigning royal family saved him. Importantly, David Higgs argues that '[r]oyal households were often said to be hothouses of homosexual behaviors' (1) and as Lobato has shown Juan Rana was often a guest of the royal family (84). The protection of Juan Rana by the royal household epitomizes Diana Fuss's 'inside / outside' theory. She explains that homosexuals simultaneously live within and outside dominant heterosexual society:

The problem, of course, with the inside/outside rhetoric, if it remains underconstructed, is that such polemics disguise the fact that most of us are inside and outside at the same time ... in order to idealize the outside we must already be, to some degree, comfortably entrenched on the inside. We really only have the leisure to idealize the subversive potential of the marginal when our place of enunciation is quite central. (5)

Obviously, within the context of the era, for Juan Rana and his 'partner in crime,' a noble page, 'place of enunciation' was of great consequence. They were sufficiently entrenched in and protected by the dominant 'inside' power circles of the day to be officiously set free after their arrest. They are a perfect example of Fuss's inside/outside theory albeit on a more life-threatening scale. Juan Rana and his accomplice were obviously quite fortunate to have escaped seemingly unscathed.

Cotarelo y Mori, Hannah E. Bergman, and Frédéric Serralta quote and make reference to this historical text each with a selective and particular interpretive slant.[8] Within Cotarelo y Mori's detailed biography of the actor only a short paragraph refers ambiguously to 'un asunto de mala especie' (shady goings-on) (clviii). The author's censured version of the original document is revealing for what it does not say. No mention is made of the reason for the arrest – the *pecado nefando* – only that the actor's involvement was minor and that he and the other accused party had been officiously set free. In eliminating any reference to the unmentionable sin, the author has suppressed the homosexuality of the actor and the main thrust of the original document. His brief account is also a perfect example of how homosexual acts were perceived as so abominable that they could not be mentioned. In contrast, Cotarelo y Mori's biography gives a detailed account of the death of Juan Rana's son in 1634, indicating that he was also a widower. Notwithstanding, what is most important for this study and, indeed, conclusive, are the many Juan Rana *entremeses* that constitute a professional, public, and flagrant confession of the actor's irregular sexuality.

Not until 1965 does any bibliographic material appear that makes further mention of Juan Rana's infamous arrest. In her book *Luis de Quiñones de Benavente y sus entremeses: Con un catálogo biográfico de los actores citados en sus obras*, Hanna E. Bergman provides the full quotation from *La corte y monarquía de España en los años de 1636 y 1637* which details the events following Juan Rana's arrest in 1636. The document's main intent – to criticize an immoral and corrupt justice system that has freed two individuals guilty of the *pecado nefando* – is thus revealed. For Bergman, however, the denial of homosexuality by the characters interpreted by Juan Rana in *Los muertos vivos* and *El pipote en nombre de Juan Rana* – two *entremeses* written by Quiñones de Benavente specifically for Juan Rana after the 1636 incident, which will be studied in chapter 4 – should be considered a public statement against false accusations of gayness brought on by his arrest. She has clearly overlooked the gay content of these *entremeses* and the fact that Juan Rana must appear to recant his gayness in front of his public.

In contrast to these works by Cotarelo y Mori and Bergman, Serralta's (1990) article 'Juan Rana Homosexual' has Juan Rana's sexuality as the central topic of discussion. The unguarded title of the article promises a more enlightened analysis of Juan Rana's sexuality. Curiously, however, while the gayness of Juan Rana's person and persona is outed in this article and important analytical tools that would have allowed for a more in-depth analysis are cited, Serralta shies away from a detailed analysis of gay content. He refuses to 'tarnish' the actor's reputation and that of the many playwrights who wrote for him. Notwithstanding Serralta's reluctance to stand by his own persuasive and conclusive findings, he does provide important analytical references and makes a useful contribution by pointing out that part of the actor's success was the result of his repertoire of 'typical' gay *gestus*. As such, his research serves as an excellent base from which to launch a more detailed and supportive analysis of Juan Rana as a gay actor.

Surprisingly this censored analytical stance towards Juan Rana's homosexuality and the importance it played in his life and career still persists among some influential critics. In her most recent book Rodríguez states:

> Como es sabido, del hecho de que aparezca en algún documento que en alguna ocasión logró evitar la cárcel pese a verse involucrado en un asunto de 'pecado nefando' algunos estudiosos han visto en Cosme Pérez determinados indicios de homosexualidad, corroborados por las constatadas y frecuentes interpretaciones de personajes afeminados, *mariones* o forzados travestismos. De todo ello sólo nos interesa que la máscara de 'Juan Rana' fuera, en efecto, una creación a partir de la mímica y la voz de Cosme Pérez (sin prejuicio del guión escrito que se viera obligado a seguir); o diríamos más, a partir de su propio cuerpo, si hemos de creer que el retrato que de él conservamos ... fuera, aparte de una resolución caricaturesca de convenciones sobre el simple o necio, un documento interpretable. (467–8)

It is documented that on one occasion or another Juan Rana managed to escape incarceration despite being involved in a case of *pecado nefando*. Because of this, some scholars have seen in Cosme Pérez definite indications of homosexuality, corroborated by his confirmed and frequent interpretations of effeminate characters, faggots, or forced transvestism. The only thing that interests us in all of this, however, is that the mask of 'Juan Rana' was, in effect, a creation based on the mimicry and the voice of Cosme Pérez (notwithstanding the written script he would have had to follow); or we might even say, based on his own body. In this latter case, much depends on whether we believe that the existing portrait of him, apart from being a product of caricatural conventions regarding the simpleton or idiot, is an interpretable document.

This critic does not consider the actor's nefarious arrest and hitherto stained reputation as an important element of his created mask, but surely it cannot be coincidental that his histrionic technique and many of the *entremeses* written for him after his arrest depended greatly on his irregular sexuality for meaning and comedic effect.

All things considered, the above-mentioned critics ignore, downplay, or simply avoid the issue of Rana's homosexuality. Fortunately, a new wave of queer scholars of the Spanish baroque period is beginning to emerge and shed some light on this hitherto ignored and misunderstood analytical territory. In the particular case of Juan Rana, José Cartagena-Calderón emphasizes the importance of Juan Rana's homosexuality and his mask:

> La sexualidad 'nefanda' de don Diego queda todavía más patente cuando en medio de una discusión éste le reprocha a su rival, don Juan: '[u]sted me tiene por rana' (Agustín Moreto *El lindo don Diego* 2319), alusión que en el contexto de esta pieza el público de entonces no hubiera tenido la menor dificultad de asociar con la figura teatral de Juan Rana. Como se sabe, Juan Rana fue el más célebre gracioso de entremeses del siglo XVII que llegó a ser identificado en las tablas por sus 'acentos y mímicas homosexuales' (Serralta, 'Juan Rana Homosexual' 85).[9] (166)

> The nefarious sexuality of Don Diego is even more obvious when in the middle of an argument he reproaches his rival, Don Juan: '[y]ou take me for a *rana* [a frog]' (Agustín Moreto *El lindo don Diego* 2319), an allusion which, in the context of this play, the public would have had no trouble at all associating with the theatrical figure of Juan Rana. As we know, Juan Rana was the most famous *gracioso* of seventeenth-century *entremeses*, who came to be known on the stage for his 'homosexual manner of speaking and acting' [Serralta, 'Juan Rana Homosexual' 85].

Indeed, in many *entremeses*, Juan Rana's homosexuality is covertly and, arguably, overtly present as a complicit basis for much of their comedic success even before his arrest. Juan Rana's arrest for the nefarious sin and subsequent quick release in 1636 outed Juan Rana in the eyes of society, but at the same time it set the stage for the evolution and refinement of his famed persona. In effect, Juan Rana's arrest served as a reinforced thematic point of departure for those who wrote for him. These playwrights took full advantage of Juan Rana's offstage double person as a base for his on-stage double persona. As such, male cross-dressing, inversion of sexual roles, and allusions to gay sexual practices were common in Juan Rana *entremeses* before and after 1636.

In the Spanish Golden Age, the *entremés* was presented between the acts of the main production and, as such, was an integral part of the seventeenth-century theatrical experience. This historical fact and, hence, the significant role that the *entremés* played during the most important period of theatre in Spain has been much overlooked by critics. The incorporation of the *entremés* within the context of the *comedia* and, indeed, of Spanish theatrical and literary history forces us to drastically change our view of Golden Age theatre as a whole. The collusion between the *entremés* and the main play paints a very different picture of hitherto perceived seventeenth-century theatre production. The *entremés* was more often than not written by a different author and produced by a separate company. For these companies and their actors, the *entremés* was their professional mainstay. Indeed, some playwrights wrote only *entremeses*. In this way, the *entremés* while an essential part of the whole must be considered as a separate entity and genre.

In microcosmic terms the *entremés* provided comic relief from the longer play. On a grander scale, however, the *entremés* served as an escape valve from the rigours of a strict and highly stratified society inasmuch as the traditional structures of power, class, and societal roles were allowed to be inverted and suspended within its represented world. The *entremés*, while performed year round, embodied the celebratory and nonrestrictive aspects of carnival. It is not surprising, therefore, that sexual activity and gender roles, two of the aspects of daily life most controlled by the religious and legal authorities of the seventeenth century, were the backbone of the *entremesil burla* or practical joke. Transvestism, inversion of sexual roles, and allusions to gay sexual practices normally restricted by officialdom were tolerated within the framework of the minicarnival *entremés*.

Humour is, of course, the main vehicle used to parody society within the *mundo al revés* or world gone topsy-turvy *entremés*. Henri Bergson has explained that laughter results from a break in continuity (66–7) or, in other words, laughter is a natural reaction to the unexpected and the unusual, surprisingly presented to the audience. This is most certainly the case in the many Juan Rana *entremeses* where sexual mores and gender identity are played with. Unmentionable body parts and their earthly functions are also a site for laughter, as Mikhail Bakhtin has noted throughout his *Rabelais and His World* (1965). The gay allusions and phallic figures aplenty in the Juan Rana *entremeses* pay homage to the bodily and bawdy humour of the medieval period that lost favour and, indeed, flavour in the eras that followed. In the *entremés*, therefore, prohibited *contra naturam* sexual acts, cross-dressing, and subversive bodily functions exaggeratedly portrayed on the one hand and semantically embedded on the other are the shtick of its parodic humour.

There is, of course, another important caustic element of humour that depends heavily on the type of audience and society to which the *entremés* is addressed:

> Pleasure – downright satisfaction – comes at the expense of some other, less fortunate soul, because we realize we are somehow better, or better off. Little people, the insecure, laugh the loudest: the smaller the ego, the higher rise to 'sudden glory.' (Sanders 9)

It can be said, therefore, that the spectator, while believing that he or she is laughing at the expense of the other, is actually laughing at him or herself. Paradoxically, therefore, the 'other,' which defines difference, marginality, censured gender, and sexual behaviour and supplies ammunition for raucous and spectacular ridicule, is an innate and ingrained part of the spectator and the society in which he or she lives. Clearly, the baroque *entremesistas* who wrote for Juan Rana were in tune with the potential that innate difference held for laughter. Significantly, these writers centred on the homosexual, the effeminate male, the masculine woman, the transvestite, and the cuckolded husband, ultimate sites for ridicule and parody of unnaturally imposed gender and sexual norms and constructs. Definitively, Juan Rana was very much a pivotal part of the societal, gender, and sexual parody that the baroque *entremés* embodied. His ambiguous identity, gender, and sexuality was perfectly in sync with the baroque perception of life and the world. Juan Rana as a person and actor ideally fitted the era's need for spectacular novelty, its obsessive questioning of the meaning of life, and indeed its *mundo al revés* perception of the world gone absurdly topsy-turvy. Juan Rana within the staged world of the *entremés* was an ingenious vehicle used to parody Spanish baroque society seen to have gone awry and to be full of inherently ambiguous and ambivalent incongruencies.

Considering the function and the prevalence of parody in the *entremés* and baroque thematic topoi, Juan Rana's homosexuality is undoubtedly an important and pivotal facet of his stage performance. As we have seen, the main sources that together form most of the existing bibliographic material on this actor – Cotarelo y Mori, Bergman, Serralta, and Rodríguez-Cuadros – conspicuously avoid the subject, dismiss his homosexuality or undermine its importance. In light of this critical reception of Juan Rana, a complete study of this actor is necessary to better understand the 'other' Spanish theatre and its place and significance within seventeenth-century Spanish theatre as a whole. The main goal of this study is, therefore, to establish the gayness of Juan Rana the actor in order to provide a more enlightened revision of seventeenth-century Spanish theatre and theatrical reception.

Apart from the historical evidence of the actor's arrest, his adopted last name Rana is in itself a key and complex indication of the actor's sexual orientation. There is no clear indication of when the actor adopted his stage name given that '[e]l sobrenombre con que le hemos designado era el ya suyo, famoso en el referido año de 1636' (Cotarelo y Mori clviii) (the famous stage name used to refer to him was already being used in the aforementioned year 1636). It would seem, therefore, that the actor had acquired his new name and identity long before being arrested for the *pecado nefando*. In other words, the gender-bending qualities of his adopted last name Rana that will be presently uncovered existed prior to his infamous arrest. This would lead to the conclusion that Juan Rana's sexuality was not revealed by his arrest but rather publicly confirmed by it.

On a purely idiomatic level, the common expression *salir rana* – literally meaning 'to result in a frog' – indicates that something or someone has turned out in a way not wished and, indeed, the end result is seen as a failure. In this sense, the actor's choice of a last name could be considered a tongue-in-cheek reference not only to his diminutive size but also to his 'erroneous' sexuality. In the same popular vein, Juan Eduardo Cirlot has shown that in legends and folktales the frog embodies the ability to change into another entity (114–15). This folk symbology of the transformable frog relates directly to acting where the assuming of various theatrical identities is fundamental. It also implies that the transmutable frog is capable of the element of surprise. On a more abstract level, however, this symbolic ability to transform could possibly be seen as Juan Rana's ability and need to modify or hide his sexual identity within a repressive and homophobic society.

On a textual level, however, Serralta shows that the actor's adopted stage name can be directly linked to homosexuality. In Luis de Belmonte Bermúdez's *Una rana hace ciento* (1657),[9] 'dos escuadras de hermosuras' (two squadrons of beauties) arrive at the banks of the Manzanares well equipped for a metaphorical fishing adventure. The banks would seem to be none other that the *tablas* (boards) on which they perform and, hence, the public is the pool from which they take their catch. This is, of course, on both the metaphorical and literal level, a natural place to encounter Juan Rana, the frog incarnate. The frog's natural swampy habitat can be directly linked to what is considered the lowly metaphorical haunts of the homosexual: 'The sodomite is frequently represented as having sunk into a filthy and bestial nature associated with dirt, mire, offal and animality' (MacFarlane 39). This coincidental aquatic and theatrical meeting allows for a series of revealing commentaries on how these women hope to get ahead in life using their many picaresque and female talents. More important, however, are the many allusions to Juan Rana's homosexuality that are found in the text.

One of the beauties announces the arrival of Juan Rana by singing, 'del humilde río sale/ una rana verdinegra,/ ni bien pescado ni carne' (183) (from the humble river comes/ a green and black frog,/ neither fish nor fowl). This is the first hint in the *entremés* of Juan Rana's in-between sexuality reinforced by his dual colouring. An ensuing dialogue between the women characters and Juan Rana continues this incriminating allusion:

RANA: Hombre soy, déme palabra
(MUJER) 2:   ¿Tú eres hombre?
RANA: ¿Pues qué?
(MUJER) 1:   Nadie:
             ni eres hombre entre los hombres,
             ni animal entre animales;
             ni eres pez entre los peces,
             ni eres ave entre las aves. (186)

RANA: I am a man, allow me to speak.
(WOMAN) 2:   You're a man?
RANA: What am I then?
(WOMAN) 1:   No one:
              you're neither a man among men,
              nor an animal among animals;
              nor a fish among fish,
              nor bird among birds.

This is, of course, a clear indication of the actor's lack of masculine qualities and his seemingly indefinable gender and being. Importantly, in this *entremés* 'ya no se le impone al personaje el más mínimo disfraz femenino' (Serralta 86) (the character is no longer given the slightest hint of a feminine costume anymore). This shows that Juan Rana does not have to be dressed up in order for his in-betweenness or homosexuality to be an essential part of his persona. The subsequent lines excluded by Serralta also give a more sexual overtone to the actor's inability to perform heterosexually:

RANA: Debo de ser cosa y cosa,
       y sin duda soy aquella
       que entra al pozo y no se moja;
       ninguno me acertará. (186)

RANA: I am no doubt one thing or another
       and without a doubt I am the one
       who enters the well but doesn't get wet;
       no one can figure me out.

Apart from the clear sexual innuendoes of these lines, Juan Rana plays with the fact that his frog persona holds the ability to puzzle through its ambiguous nature. But as Serralta has indicated, Juan Rana is as interested as his lady friends in 'making a catch' (86):

RANA: ¿Y saben lo que se pescan?
(MUJER) 2:   Hombres.
RANA: Pues en buena parte
             están; miren cómo bullen
             en las olas del estanque.
             ¡Anzuelos al agua, anzuelos!
             por uno que me saquen
             daré un doblón. (185)

RANA: Do you know what you are fishing for?
(WOMAN) 2:   Men.
RANA: Well, they're there;
             see how they make bubbles
             in the waves of the pond.
             Hooks in the water, hooks!
             for each one you fish out
             I'll give you a doubloon.

Juan Rana's willingness to pay the women if they can reel in a man from the public pool of men seated in front of them eliminates any notion of sexual ambiguity.

Yet another indication of Juan Rana's homosexuality overlooked by Serralta is Juan Rana's self-acclaim that he is 'Orfeo de las aguas' (185) (Orpheus of the waters) in the play. Apart from the obvious reference to Juan Rana's many singing parts, the well-known Orpheus myth is considered by some authorities to be symbolic of homosexuality:

> The death of Orpheus has given rise to a large number of traditions. It was generally said that he was killed by the women of Thrace, but the reasons behind this are many and various. Sometimes the women resent his fidelity to the memory of Eurydice, interpreting it as an insult to themselves. It was also said that Orpheus wanted to have nothing to do with women and surrounded himself with young men: it was even suggested that he was the inventor of pederasty and that his lover was Calais, son of Boreas. (Grimal 332)

While the homosexual interpretation is but one of many interpretations of the Orpheus myth, the other indications of this *entremés* would lead us to believe that Juan Rana's mythological self-acclamation alludes to his other sexuality. It also cannot be overlooked that Juan Rana's partner was a young page – a further pederast parallel with the Orpheus myth.

Ultimately, the analysis of the actor's adopted stage name shows that there is, indeed, much in a name. From a folkloric, idiomatic, textual, and mythical standpoint the actor's stage-name Rana is a meaningful reference to his 'irregular' sexuality that existed prior to his arrest. Like the symbolically ambiguous animal categorization of the amphibious frog, the name Juan Rana embodies an in-betweenness or, in other words, homosexuality. In this way, the study of the historical data and the implications of the Rana name form a strong base for the analysis of the Juan Rana *entremeses*.

The examination of Juan Rana's adopted last name shows that his multifarious mask was thematically based on his person. And while his homosexuality would seem to be common knowledge, it nonetheless had to be performed in seemingly covert fashion. The ambiguous manner in which the amphibious Juan Rana persona is presented represents the how and why of the actor's success. In camouflaging Juan Rana's well-known sexuality behind a transparent guise of ambiguity, the *entremesistas* and the production managers were testing the limits not only of theatre but also of society itself. This study of the Juan Rana person/persona is divided into three chapters and while each centres on a different facet of ambiguity, all ambiguous aspects of the mask are interconnected and interwoven. As such, Juan Rana's on- and offstage ambiguity is studied as an interacting continuum of complexity.

The physical and artistic onstage appearance of other Juan Ranas is the first aspect of ambiguity analysed in chapter 2, 'The Self-"Reflective" Juan Rana: Acting, Meaning, Being the Double/*Doppelgänger*.' From a theoretic standpoint, both Albert Guerard and Carl Francis Keppler consider the double too vague and ambiguous as used in literary criticism. Keppler ultimately rejects the double and its well-established counterparts. It would seem ironic that the argument of these theorists against the use of the double centres on its literary raison d'être. The double has from its inception been used as a means to interpret the unexplainable and, more important to this study, to tantalizingly express that which cannot be explicitly revealed. Accordingly, it must be ambiguous and its great power as a rhetorical figure rests in its vagueness. For this reason, the double remains a valid literary term for this study. Andrew J. Webber delineates the main properties of the *Doppelgänger* in his introduction to *The Dopplegänger: Double Visions in German Literature* (1996). His theory that the *Doppelgänger* must create a double vision, which in turn causes double-talk, is of particular importance to the study of Juan Rana. Otto Rank and René Girard's work on the double adds an ethnological angle to the Juan Rana doubling effect.

In the *entremeses* studied in this chapter, *El triunfo de Juan Rana* (Calderón de la Barca 1670), *Los dos Juan Ranas* (Moreto y Cavana 1675), *Juan Ranilla* (Cáncer y Velasco 1676), *El retrato de Juan Rana* (Villaviciosa 1663), *La loa de Juan Rana* (Moreto y Cavana 1664), sundry physical and artistic manifestations of Juan Rana appear. It would, at first, seem paradoxical and, indeed, odd that duplicates of a one-of-a-kind *gracioso* should flourish in the works of different *entremesistas*. However, these Juan Ranas demonstrate a clever use of a long-standing European theatrical tradition. The existence of Juan Rana doubles shows that the Juan Rana mask had a life of its own in a manner consistent with the commedia dell'arte tradition. Unlike the historic character types of commedia dell'arte, however, the persona coexisted with its originator. In taking full advantage of this unique coexistence, the *entremesistas* ultimately concocted a staged and stirring cocktail of illusion and reality. The coexistence of the inventor and his own invented mask allow for perplexing and parodic encounters that test preconceived ideas of reality. This unique use of the doubling mask represents an ingenious twist on a long-standing theatrical tradition. And while this analytical bent allows for a metaphysical questioning of reality itself, it simultaneously cements and perpetuates the ambiguous nature of Juan Rana. It would seem, therefore, that the singularity of Juan Rana is based on duplication and, indeed, duplicity.

The strict and confining dress codes of the baroque era and Juan Rana's cross-dressing violations of them are examined in chapter 3, 'Crossing the Gendered "Clothes"-Line.' While clothes can be considered our second skin their purpose goes beyond the mere practical protection of the body. Jean E. Howard explains that in seventeenth-century Europe clothes were a means of dividing and controlling society but, more important for this study, they denoted a gender differentiation that ensured a division of labour in favour of men (23). Cross-dressing is, therefore, a serious threat to societal order and control and, indeed, of the time-honoured male/female dyad. More specifically, the donning of female garb by a man represents not only a self-imposed loss of privileged status but also an aberration of masculinity. As Lesley Ferris has shown, the cross-dressing male actor has caused societal malaise since Plato's time; in subverting primordial sexual and gender constructs all civil and personal liminality can be seen as mutable (9). Gail Bradbury's insightful study of the Spanish Golden Age's fascination with irregular sexuality and its manifestations in the *comedia* adds decisive historical and literary strength to this chapter's examination of Juan Rana.

The study of Juan Rana's roles as Woman in the *entremeses* studied in this chapter, *La boda de Juan Rana*, *Juan Rana muger* (Cáncer y Velasco 1676) and *El parto de Juan Rana* (Lanini y Sagredo c. 1660), challenges the constrictive foundation of the baroque engendered dress code. The defiant subversion indicative of these *entremeses* represents an acute condemnation of the oppression of women and of all others in the baroque era. Its exposure of the inequalities inherent in a phallocentric society remains operative for our own seemingly advanced time.

Up to this point in the study, the visual and the semantic can be considered equal partners in yielding the desired parodic ambiguity. In chapter 2 the 'visual compulsion' (Webber 3) of the double/*Doppelgänger* operates in tandem with the many semantic double entendres played on the Juan Rana person and persona. Similarly, the cross-dressed Juan Rana and the accompanying wordplay interact as a shocking means of achieving 'sudden glory.' In other words, the visual effect, be it seen or read, coexists with the interpretation of puns and wordplay and vice versa. Each maintained an autonomous ability to induce laughter. However, in chapter 4, '"Mas apetezco fuentes que braseros": Phallic Innuendoes and Confessions,' the visual is shown not to possess the capacity to produce laughter independently. The visual only becomes comical and, indeed, logical when semantic double meanings register in the mind of the play-goer. Only then does it act as a comedic enhancer. Ultimately, the spectator's understanding of the parodic supersedes his or her seeing of it.

In the initial four *entremeses* studied in chapter 4, *El desafío de Juan Rana* (Calderón de la Barca 1669–70), *Los muertos vivos, El mundo al revés* (Quiñones de Benavente 1653), and *Las fiestas del aldea* (Bernardo de Quirós 1656), phallic symbols and homosexual innuendoes that demand semantic and, indeed, complicit knowledge on the part of the receptor are employed. More precisely, weaponry and especially the sword are used as phallic symbols. The fencing soldier, therefore, is understood to be a metaphor for homosexual activity. With each *entremés* the homosexual innuendoes become progressively infused with details that reflect Juan Rana's personal *pecado nefando* past. In the last *entremés* of this chapter, *El pipote en nombre de Juan Rana* (Quiñones de Benavente c. 1660), the infusion becomes complete. Here, an overview of Juan Rana's acting career is combined with bellicose imagery and the recounting of a late-night encounter with a sword-wielding young man. Their symbolic swordplay would seem to reenact and mock the incident that led up to Juan Rana's 'incriminating' arrest. Juan Rana's acting career and bellicose imagery are definitely tied together to detail the actor's on-stage and offstage homosexuality. However, without the element of complicity and topical knowledge of the person/persona of Juan Rana on the part of the spectator, the phallic imagery and homosexual allusions lie flat – they have no meaningful or comedic value.

The most important treatise of the baroque era on the art of writing drama demonstrates the significance that interpreting semantic difference held for the era's play-goer and, accordingly, advocates the creation of a complicit audience. In *El arte nuevo de hacer comedias en este tiempo* (1609), Lope de Vega y Carpio explains how a specific type of ambiguity can be used to fashion a complicit public. He makes reference to 'incertidumbre anfibológica' as one of the pivotal means of pleasing his patrons (212). Lope de Vega's mention of 'amphibolic uncertainty' refers specifically to ambiguity achieved through double meanings, uncertain and equivocal grammatical constructions, phrases, and proposals, or, in general terms, the ambiguous use of language. He insightfully

understood that his paying public delighted in the equivocal and amphibolic nature of language and that each individual play-goer revelled at
the idea that only he or she was in on the joke. Creating this amphibolic
illusion in the play-goer was a means of assuring the success of the
theatrical production. It is clear that Lope de Vega's keen grasp of the
baroque audience's psyche unequivocally promotes amphibology as an
effective means of winning the spectator over. It would seem that the
entremesistas studied in this chapter were particularly aware of this winning and complicit principle.

In the final chapter, 'The Triumphant Juan Rana,' the significance of
Juan Rana's unprecedented success and fame based on his ambiguous
and amphibolic portrayal of homosexuality is reaffirmed. The analysis of
the Juan Rana *entremeses* as they relate to the questions of gender, sex,
phallocentrism, language, and gayness is considered vital for an enlightened perception of Golden Age theatre as a whole. The reconstruction
of the actor and the person brings the importance of his gayness out of
the closet; Juan Rana's gay performance is brought back to centre stage
as initially performed in the seventeenth-century Spanish theatre. From
an analytical standpoint this chapter emphasizes that gay acting was the
quintessential carnivalesque 'gaiety' initially intended by the seventeenth-
century *entremesistas* who wrote specifically for Juan Rana. The ramifications of Juan Rana's in-betweenness are further developed to show that
they hold emblematic importance for the baroque historical period as a
whole.

2 The Self-'Reflective' Juan Rana: Acting, Meaning, Being the Double/*Doppelgänger*

Pedro Calderón de la Barca called Juan Rana the 'máximo gracioso' of the Golden Age *entremés*.[1] This extraordinary tribute by one of the greatest playwrights of the Spanish Golden Age heralds the singularity of Juan Rana's created persona, the uniqueness of his acting ability, and the longevity of his career. Many other great *entremesistas* who wrote specifically for him included Luis de Belmonte Bermúdez, Francisco Bernardo de Quirós, Gerónimo de Cáncer y Velasco, Augustín Moreto y Cavana, Luis Quiñones de Benavente, and Sebastián de Villaviciosa. They also believed that only one actor in this era was capable of his histrionic onstage antics. His adoring public, which included everyone from the lowly *mosqueteros* to the reigning royal family, shared this opinion. It has been said that his mere entrance on stage was enough to make the audience as a whole go into hysterics (Cotarelo y Mori clxi). No doubt Juan Rana was also a great favourite with the era's *autores*, or producers, as the mere inclusion of his famed name in the *entremés* title assured a respectable level of success for the theatrical event as a whole. It is no surprise, therefore, that many of the over fifty *entremeses* written for Juan Rana include his name in their title. All things considered, Juan Rana was definitively a one-of-a-kind actor and, ultimately, a major drawing card for and a great asset to Spanish Golden Age theatre.

Given this unique status, it would seem at first quite paradoxical that other Juan Ranas would frequently appear in many Juan Rana-specific *entremeses*. These doubles appeared in many guises – other actors playing the Juan Rana mask alongside him, artistic reproductions and mirror images of the actor. It is striking that different *entremesistas* returned over and over to the double when writing for Juan Rana. Why was it that this particular rhetorical figure was considered so suited to this famous and unique *gracioso?* How could it be that the uniqueness of an actor and his persona should foster so many theatrical doubles? The answer inevitably lies in the inherent qualities of the double, a rhetorical figure much like the complex and seemingly simple on- and offstage Juan Rana.

The double is one of the oldest rhetorical figures, acquiring a time-honoured status in the annals of rhetoric. First Nation and Middle Eastern beliefs, Greek mythology, Neoplatonic concepts, nineteenth-century German literature, and modern physiology and psychiatry abound with references to the double in its various manifestations. The double remains a powerful and complex literary device that maintains its ability to fascinate and perplex the contemporary receptor and theorist alike. Theorists continue to wrestle with the double as a concept as Albert Guerard complains:

> The word *double* is embarrassingly vague, as used in literary criticism. It need not imply autoscopic or even close physical resemblance ... Characters who seem occultly connected in the author's imagination (and such connection may take many forms) may also be referred to as doubles. A minor character may reenact a major character's traumatic experience, if only because the author could not leave the trauma alone. A strong feeling of sympathetic identification may lead to a sense of doubleness, an immobilizing recognition of the self one might have been. (3)

For this critic the many vague interpretations of the double prevent serious and clear analysis. Perhaps for this same reason Carl Francis Keppler completely rejects the double and other related literary terms. Labelling such terms as the double, *Doppelgänger*, and inner self as misleading, Keppler adopts the 'second self' as a more acceptable expression. For him it 'suggests twofoldness without implying duplication and like the "inner self" it suggests a deeper relationship but not one that is confined to a state of mind' (3). Guerard's remarks on the double and Keppler's rejection of well-established double terms shed light on the inherent complexity of defining and using the double as a literary figure. It would seem, however, that these two theorists have forgotten the essential raison d'être of the double.

On the one hand, the double is used to represent the unexplainable of nature and life, that which would seem to be the work of a higher being. More specifically for our purposes, the double tantalizingly refers openly, surreptitiously, or subversively to moral, political, sexual, and other social matters that cannot be openly expressed for reasons of good taste or for fear of chastisement. As such the double must be inherently ambiguous. Quite obviously the double holds great potential and is the perfect site for parody and satire, as is the case for Juan Rana. While Guerard and Keppler's arguments are valid for what they reveal of the frustrations of defining and using the theory of the double, it would not seem useful to reject well-known terms for this literary and real-life phenomenon. In other words, no renaming of the double and its related terms can eliminate the fact that the double embodies ambiguity and, at times, is problematic for analysis. In this study, therefore, two well-known literary terms are employed – the double and the *Doppelgänger*.[2] The first term refers to this phenomenon in a general sense, while the latter designates a physical, artistic onstage presence of a Juan Rana double. Ultimately, both terms embody unavoidable ambiguity – it is the nature of this literary beast and, indeed, of the dubious Juan Rana.

The double, in the case of Juan Rana, is also a vehicle for boisterous, bawdy, carnivalesque, and gut-wrenching humour. Laughter is enjoyed at the expense of Juan Rana and his persona and so he becomes the quintessential baroque scapegoat. René Girard in his study of the double identifies the scapegoat as 'an outlet for violence [who] unif[ies] the entire community against him' (104). As such the actor as a ritual victim dies onstage for the common good. This is particularly true of the comedic actor:

> The loss of autonomy and self-possession that is present in all forms of comic must be present, somehow, in laughter itself. Laughter, in other words, must never be very different from whatever causes it. Scenes in which the laughing spectator is included are invariably circular. The culprit is getting his just desserts. The retributive justice is no idealistic illusion; it is the reality of the structure. He who laughs last laughs best. (128)

The audience in its collective laughter feels superior and is cleansed of the social evils that the scapegoat is seen to embody. Juan Rana's doubles live up to the time-honoured status of this dynamic and complex rhetorical device.

To analyse the complexity of the Juan Rana doubles it is necessary, therefore, to consider various aspects of the double while keeping in mind the importance of its use as *entremesil* comic relief from the main production and from life itself. Onstage artistic and physical doubles, combined with what can be considered mental imaginations of the onstage Juan Rana, are analysed for both ambiguous doubleness and cathartic jocularity. Consequently, the different facets of the double, ancient and modern, visual and psychological, must be combined in order to analyse the duplicitous and comical nature of Juan Rana be it his person, his persona, or a combination of the two.

Pedro Calderón de la Barca wrote *El triunfo de Juan Rana* as a tribute to the longevity and successful career of Juan Rana. Born near the turn of the century, Juan Rana died in 1672, three months after acting in *El triunfo*, his last royal command performance (Greer and Varey 42). *El triunfo* was included in *Fieras afemina amor* (1670), one of Calderón's grandiose mythological plays staged at court.[3] As such, the *entremés* was a fitting place for Calderón to crown the actor 'el máximo gracioso' of the *entremés*. Clearly at the time of the writing of *El triunfo* both men had long since reached the pinnacle of success and been celebrated in their respective professions.[4] Logically, both the play and the *entremés* become an ideal site for celebrating and reflecting on fame, life, and, of course, 'life as a dream.' On the one hand, Calderón's *El triunfo* is a theatrical celebration of Juan Rana but it also serves as a contrast to *Fieras* and makes intertexual references to his famous *La vida es sueño* (1636). Ultimately, the playwright carefully orchestrates many levels of perceived reality inside and outside the confines of this *entremés* and in doing so gives a new and complex spin on his celebrated theme, 'life as a dream.'

Significantly, *Fieras* marks a turning point in Calderón's career and life: 'Después, entonces, de un largo vacío en su producción dramática, Calderón entra, con *Fieras afemina amor*, en su último período, el de su vejez' (Varey and Shergold 40, in Wilson 17) (After a long break in his dramatic writing, Calderón enters, with *Fieras afemina amor*, his last period, that of his old age). This elaborate and complicated work by a mature and courtly Calderón was not conceived as a popular performance, as its many components and lengthy dramatis personae demanded a production on a grand and expensive scale. 'As the lengthy stage directions show, the performance was on a magnificent scale ... It is clear ... an attempt was made to surpass earlier plays in the amount of lavish ostentation which was used' (Wilson 18). Indeed, 'it was ideal for a grand occasion, when expense was no object and two companies of actors could collaborate' (20). When the play was finally staged as a *fiesta palaciega* in celebration of the third birthday of Princess María Antonia, with the royal family and foreign dignitaries in attendance,[5] the production proved to be financially and logistically challenging:[6]

Estas diversions teatrales son muy costosas; por la documentación que ha sobrevivido sobre la representación en 1672 de *Fieras afemina amor* podemos hacernos una idea de su riqueza y atractivo para el público y de su coste, a pesar de que no disponemos de todos los documentos y cuentas sobre su presta en escena. Esta documentación muestra las dificultades a que se enfrenta la burocracia para poder satisfacer la demanda y encontrar la financiación necesaria para estas obras de gran espectáculo, y expone la manera en que los problemas económicos del país se reflejan en el microcosmos de las diversiones teatrales. Detrás de los lujosos cuadros teatrales están los oscuros burócratas, haciendo sus difíciles maniobras para que siga la representación y no se rompa la armonía musical. El teatro de Corte es, en otro sentido más, el reflejo de la realidad de la Espana de los Austrias y de la primera década del siglo XVIII. (Greer and Varey 78–9)

These theatrical diversions are very costly; according to the documentation that has survived about the 1672 production of *Fieras afemina amor* we can get an idea of its opulence and appeal for the public and its expense, despite not having all the documents and receipts of its staging. This documentation shows the difficulties that public servants face in satisfying the demand and finding the necessary financing for these works on a grand scale, and reveals the way in which the country's economic problems are reflected in the microcosmos of theatrical diversions. Behind the scenes of the luxurious theatrical stagings are the overlooked bureaucrats, carrying out difficult manoeuvers so that the show might go on and the musical harmony not be broken. The theatre of the court is, in another sense, the reflection of the reality of Spain under the House of Austria and of the first decade of the eighteenth century.

Quite obviously Charles II favoured the staging of *Fieras* regardless of the expense and complexities of its production. This perceived need by Charles II to show his magnificence though grandiose spectacle coincides with Larry F. Norman's historical explanation of the 'theatrical baroque':

As feudalism and its attendant dispersion of power died away, new centralized courts sought to increase their sway over the public's imagination with propaganda campaigns that equaled that of the Counter-Reformation Church. And again, nothing advertised their magnificence so well as dramatic spectacles. Presented both outside and indoors, in splendid gardens or palatial halls, court festivities allied the theatrical elements of costumes, sets and stage machinery, and mythological stories with the traditions of jousting games, processions, and court balls. (3–4)

As *El triunfo* is an integral part of this major production and show of royal power, Juan Rana must have been quite highly considered by Calderón, the king, and the play's select audience. The particular veneration held for the actor by Calderón becomes clear in an analysis of the *entremés* in the context of the main play and in relation to *La vida es sueño*.

Fieras is set in the far-flung, mythological land of Libya, and Hercules is its main character. The protagonist, however, is not represented as the typical mythological semigod hero known for his masculine prowess and greatness.[7] Instead, the humanized Hercules is portrayed as a violent and savage man who listens to the wisdom of none and spreads havoc and death wherever he treads. In the course of the play, he kills the Libyan king and the future husband and true love of Princess Yole. Considering this pejorative and damning characterization, it is not surprising that Hercules is headed for a fall from the onset of *Fieras*. It is the maltreated Yole with the assistance of the Graces, Cupid and Venus, who finally forces Hercules to see the ugly truth about himself and to come to the realization that he has acted wrongly.

One of Hercules' greatest faults is his denial and rejection of love. He is shown by Yole and her supernatural helpers that one cannot deny the force of love, an integral part of being human. Finally, the humanized Hercules is forced to succumb and submit to love, albeit an unattainable goal in this instance; Yole, the woman he is magically made to love, will not have him. Hercules' long and emotional journey to self-realization does not represent a typical Herculean triumph but rather 'a plea for humane conduct to women and an attack on the old-fashioned attitude towards them. But in its most powerful sense it is the story of a man who discovers himself and better values as the plot unfolds' (Wilson 46). *El triunfo* in its celebration of Juan Rana's life and career represents a remarkable counterstudy to Calderón's Hercules and the play as a whole.

Surprisingly, Edward M. Wilson states that *El triunfo* would 'appear to have little connection with the play itself; perhaps [its] function was simply a contrast with it (25). But if the *entremés* contrasts with *Fieras*, does it not serve an important function in relation to the main play? Indeed, this work of *teatro breve* within the confines of the *fiesta palaciega* reinforces the play's finale and main theme spoken by Cupid at the end of the first act: 'Ninguno vencerse pudo a sí mesmo' (109) (No man alone has ever himself controlled) or as Wilson interprets: 'Man only behaves reasonably if he obeys forces like divine Grace or Love which control from outside the anarchy of his desires' (46). In doing so, *El triunfo* strengthens Cupid's foreshadowing words and gives the audience another perspective on one of the central themes of the main play, fame. The search for fame is a central theme in *Fieras* as the physical staging of the play demonstrates:

> There was on it [the proscenium] a 'caballo con alas' [winged horse], which, though ridden by Mercury, alludes also to Hércules's victory over the Herperian dragon at the beginning of Act III and his borrowing of the horse from the Muses at the end of the second act. More important than these forward-looking allusions is the idea of *fama*, which was closely associated with Pegasus by the mythographers. *Fama* will be one of the themes of the play. (Wilson 25)

As the play unfolds, however, it becomes clear that Hercules' actions represent a gratuitous and irresponsible pursuit of fame. His search represents a model of how one should not act. Hercules' negative model in his blind search for fame is in direct contrast to the already famous Juan Rana celebrated in *El triunfo*.

El triunfo in its entirety is about achieved fame and not the misguided search for it; the *entremés* celebrates the greatness of the now aged and retired Juan Rana. Juan Rana's celebrity was never that of a hero, as is the case of the mythological Hercules. His star status was based on the fact that he embodied the unheroic characteristics of the consummate fool. In general terms, Juan Rana's success was based on a stereo-theatrical persona. The spectator of this period was well accustomed to his persona and expected to see and experience a well-established and defined mode of histrionic behaviour as Evangelina Rodríguez notes (566). Juan Rana, as a true *gracioso*, represented the weak, feeble-minded, and laughable *chivo expiatorio*. He also personified the unworldly country bumpkin, an *entremesil* topos that easily delighted the urban theatre audience. As noted before, apart from his rustic attire and *gestus*, Juan Rana's histrionic social position of inferiority was verbally portrayed through his farcical rural dialect. In this vein, Juan Rana misinterpreted and misused language, just like the bumbling and gullible buffoon that he played would. In contrast to Hercules' ultimate demise as an antihero of human proportions, Juan Rana's well-known antiheroism has made him an exemplary cause célèbre. *El triunfo* and its inclusion in the *Fieras* embrace Juan Rana's antiheroism; the *entremés* is the celebration of humanness and making the best of one's situation in life. Juan Rana becomes Hercules' alter egó and this semigod referencing adds to the main goal of *El triunfo*, the apotheosis of Juan Rana. Significantly, there exists an important aspect of Juan Rana's on- and offstage life that also plays an important part in Calderón's contrasting of Juan Rana and Hercules.

Juan Rana achieved success and acquired fame by playing on and, indeed, playing up what for many is considered a great defect, his homosexuality, his 'unmanliness.' It would seem by the success that followed his 1636 arrest and liberation that his other sexuality and marginal societal status as an *entremesil* actor gave those who wrote for him a venue to compose numerous critical works about society that otherwise would not have been allowed. Juan Rana as a pint-size theatrical fool known to be a homosexual represents a nonthreatening entity from a gender, sexual, and societal perspective. His marginal status became the main thematic source for the many *entremeses* written specifically for him. One such theme was the unjust status and treatment of women in society, which not coincidentally is one of the main themes of *Fieras* as Don W. Cruickshank has adeptly shown. Undoubtedly, one of the most 'shocking' and comic means to deliver an antimisogynist message is through male to female cross-dressing as Juan Rana did in other *entremesil* performances.[8]

Juan Rana's theatrical cross-dressing *entremeses* evoked the subversive questioning of sex and gender roles. While this theatrical practice is not specifically mentioned in *El triunfo*, it is common knowledge that cross-dressing and other unmanly characterizations were an integral part of the Juan Rana persona. Once again a parallel can be drawn with Calderón's Hercules. In the first act of the *Primera jornada* Hercules complains in a long harangue about the weakness that succumbing to love represents. Hercules specifically alludes to Achilles' fateful and distasteful cross-dressing for love:

> Y cuando no hubiera tantos
> ejemplares como cuentan
> del tiempo el buril en bronces,
> de la Fama el bronce en lenguas,
> de alto héroes que afearon
> la grata faz de suprema

opinión con el lunar
de que el amor los divierta,
el de Aquiles me bastar[a]
no más, para aborrezca
amor y mujer, cuando oigo
cuán vil por Deidamia bella
vistió femeniles ropas,
peinando el cabello a trenzas; (91)

Even if there were not so many
examples told
by the chiselled bronze of Fame
where words reverberate,
of lofty heroes who disfigured
the pleasing face of supreme
opinion with the blemish
with which love should amuse them,
that of Achilles alone would suffice
for me to abhor
love and woman, when I hear
how ignobly he for beautiful Deidamia
donned feminine garments,
arranging his hair in tresses;

Hercules disdainfully believes that giving over to the power of love will result in being weak like a woman and, to a certain degree, becoming a woman as symbolized by Achilles' disgraceful donning of female garb. But Hercules is forced to cross-dress as the ultimate humiliation in his self-examination and transformation into the prolove antihero:

> Hércules falls asleep, exhausted by the struggle with Anteo and by the emotional battle that he has gone through. Yole's moment for revenge has come. She calls on the others to help her to kill Hércules in vengeance for her dead father and dead husband. Herperia persuades her to revenge herself in another way. They replace his club by a distaff, and comb and dress his hair like a woman's. They call the soldiers to witness their general's humiliation ... He vainly begs to be spared the shame of being seen in this state by his men, but Yole and the Graces are adamant. His army sees him prostrate and in tears at Yole's feet. (Wilson 36)

Unlike Calderón's Hercules, who is literally brought to his knees and tragically forced to cross-dress by women as a form of punishment and as a humiliating show of surrender, Juan Rana's theatrical cross-dressing is a wilful and comic act in favour of women; many of the *entremeses* in which he starred portrayed the injustices women had to endure. *El triunfo* mirrors in a celebratory manner not only the life and career of Juan Rana but also the part he played in the fight for women's rights and a better society. It is in the *entremés*, therefore, that the audience is presented not only with a prowomen message but also with a nobler and truer way of achieving fame and being true to oneself.[9] Curiously enough, in *Fieras* Calderón's Hercules kills the Nemean lion and in doing so unwittingly does a favour to Music, Beauty, and Wit; his gratuitous killing of the lion frees the Graces from danger. In contrast, Juan Rana's life and career is presented as a deliberate and heroic celebration of the arts and the equality of the sexes. The actor is kept from danger not by an act of violence but rather by the royal family and the theatre community that supported him. In writing and staging his triumphant *entremés*, Calderón was clearly one of Juan Rana's great supporters.

Calderón further displays his respect for Juan Rana and indeed bestows the greatest of compliments on him by linking *El triunfo* to his most celebrated play, *La vida es sueño*. This play is beyond doubt an early and monumental triumph that shaped and defined Calderón's long and illustrious life and career. The playwright, fully aware of the play's importance, positioned it 'as the lead play in the first volume of his collected works (1636) ... In addition, he capitalized on its popularity by twice allegorizing it as *autos sacramentales*' (de Armas 3). In *El triunfo* the aged and famous Calderón once again exploits his dream theme; the long-lasting popularity and fame of his masterpiece is remoulded to fit *El triunfo*. Parodic intertexual references to *La vida es sueño* are as central to the success of *El triunfo de Juan Rana* as its contrast to *Fieras*. The *entremés* provides the audience with the unique opportunity to experience the elder Calderón's rethinking of the play and its main theme from a temporal and more experienced distance. The end result is an intriguing retake on the dream theme and reality itself.

Dreams have fascinated, intrigued, dismayed, and terrified human beings from what would seem the beginning of time. Much importance has been given to the transcendental value of dreams. This cerebral world of slumber reconstructed at best in a juxtaposed and jumbled manner in the waking hours has been interpreted by religious and literary groups as an ominous glimpse into the other world or a prophetic preview of things to come. In the baroque era, as Manuel Aguirre has noted, dreams were seen to mirror 'the unreality in waking life; as if to counterbalance this, the unreal dream is used as a symbol to affirm and stress the splendor and lightness of the ephemeral, and to 'relativize' death itself' (4). Calderón's *La vida es sueño* exemplifies the era's fixation with illusory reality and the world beyond and, hence, the disquieting fears of our waking hours. Accordingly, Calderón's concept of the dream is not the product of physical sleep, as in other interpretations of the oneiric, but rather a disquieting interpretation of life itself seen to parallel the incongruent qualities typical of dreams. While presented in a much different manner, the basic conditions of the life-as-a-dream theme are the same in *El triunfo*, and the ultimate message is as grand and far-reaching in scope.

In *El triunfo* a statue of Juan Rana has been commissioned to honour the actor's great achievements and to assure that his fame lives on after his death. Prior to his physical entrance onstage, however, an obvious intertexal reference is made to *La vida es sueño*. In the opening lines of *El triunfo* two men hysterically run on and off the stage announcing that the offstage Escamilla – also a famous baroque *gracioso* – is having problems staying on his mount. From the wings Escamilla bellows:

Hipogrifo violento,
mira que eres un mísero jumento,
y no toca a tu estilo el desbocarte;
¡jo, burro!, no te empeñes en matarte. (113)

Violent gryphon,
you are a wretched ass,
and to bolt does not become you;
Oh, donkey! Don't insist on killing yourself.

As Wilson has explained, this passage is 'an example of Calderón's fondness for self-parody. Escamilla calls his bolting ass "hipogrifo violento," the lofty, florid term used by the honour-seeking Rosaura at the beginning of *La vida es sueño*, but then descends to the homely, direct terms "mísero jumento" and "pollino" (jackass)' (236 note 1456). Like Rosaura, Escamilla eventually falls off his horse but instead of metaphorically bloodying himself or breaking a rib as he had feared, he remains unharmed. Two men unceremoniously '*sacan a Escamilla en hombros, con botas, espuelas y demás aderezos de camino* (sd 113) (carry Escamilla out on their shoulders, who is wearing boots, spurs, and other travelling accoutrements). When asked the reason for his great hurry, Escamilla explains that

... hoy en el Retiro
ha de haber una cosa
tan nueva, tan terrible, tan grandiosa,
tan mucha, tan horrenda,
tan, tan, tan, tan, tan, tan, tan estupenda,
que por verla, ese asno y yo en cuadrilla
postas corrimos hoy desde la Villa,
aunque tan recia carrera ha sido
que también por la posta hemos caído ... (114)

... today in the Retiro
there will be a thing
so new, so terrible, so grandiose,
so great, so horrendous,
so, so, so, so, so, so, so stupendous,
that to see it, this ass and I in stages
hurried today from the city,
though such a swift pace has caused
us also to fall in our haste.

Escamilla considers his trip to have been difficult but, in truth, he has only made his way from the city to the Retiro. Unlike Rosaura, therefore, he has not undertaken a gruelling voyage from a far-off land to revenge his honour or anything of the kind. His short trip is for another reason – to see an effigy of Juan Rana. Obviously, this opening scene is a deliberate parody of one of Calderón's more memorable and famous stage images. We can only imagine the pleasure the playwright took in writing this opening spoof and the delight the audience took in recognizing and witnessing it. With this hippogriffical opening scene, Calderón's intentions of self-referential parody are evident.

Presently, this extraordinary 'cosa' made reference to by Escamilla appears onstage. It is none other than Juan Rana. If Escamilla was unceremoniously brought onto the stage, Juan Rana's entrance is quite the opposite. Two men carry Juan Rana onstage as an actor/statue, each bearing the typical symbols of his mask, a staff and a tunic: '*Tocan cajas y trompetas, y sale Juan Rana en un carro triunfal, con mucho acompañamiento, y (a)delante dos hombres, uno con el sayo y otro con la vara'* (sd 115) (Drums and trumpets sound and Juan Rana is brought onstage on a triumphal float, with great accompaniment, at the front of which come two men, one carrying the tunic and the other carrying the staff). His entrance, one could say, is befitting a king, albeit the king of comedy. This appearance of Juan Rana causes great onstage excitement. Apart from the fact that he was a celebrity, the actor ' ... en su casa vive retirado,/ negado a acclamations del tablado ...' (115) (lives at home retired,/ denied the acclamations of the stage). In real life, Juan Rana had lived in secluded retirement for some time and returned to the stage solely by royal command. The actor's health must have been fragile as he was unable to walk and passed away three months after the performance. Hence for reasons of frailty, Juan Rana had to be carried onstage (236 note 1508). Notwithstanding, within the created world of the stage, Juan Rana, like Segismundo (the protagonist of *La vida es sueño*), has been keep away from public view and his reappearance is a fêted event. In *La vida es sueño*'s preplay history, Segismundo was secretly and quickly whisked away at birth from the royal court to a prison by his father, the king of Poland. By doing so, the king believes he is forestalling the horrific actions he foresees his son performing. In the actual play, Segismundo as an imprisoned young man contemplates the meaning of life and bemoans his dreadful existence. In a moment of paternal weakness, Segismundo is returned to court and, as predicted, carries out terrible acts. Although taken back to his prison in a poison-induced stupor by his fearful father, Segismundo is in due course returned to court by the people wishful for a direct heir to the throne. This abrupt back and forward between two extreme states of being causes Segismundo to question reality, consider the consequences of one's actions, ponder the unpredictability of existence, and ultimately, wonder if life is a dream. In the end, Segismundo acts in a just and regal manner towards his family and the people, thus showing that the future cannot be foreseen or controlled by man. The royal family and foreign dignitaries present at this lavish production would have assuredly enjoyed this intertexual reference and the irony of Juan Rana's regal entrance. As the *entremés* unfolds, however, the royal family, itself a spectacle of power, is woven into the *entremés*'s plot.

Onstage, a crowd of actors and musicians follows Juan Rana's triumphant procession intermittently yelling, '¡Viva Juan Rana!' (Long live Juan Rana!), '¡Viva sin desvelo!' (May he live without worries!), '¡Viva hasta que la rana tenga pelo!' (May he live forever!), 'Viva Juan Rana más que vive Cribas!' (May he live longer than Christ!). They can be seen to represent the theatre community and his admiring public. At the same time, however, their exuberant exclamations support the notion of a majestic entry. Presently a 'man' appears demanding Juan Rana's statue on behalf of the goddess Fame:

> ¡Dios la dé su gracia,
> y a mí, par que la lleve!
> Que de parte de la Fama
> vengo por ella, porque
> quiero luego colocarla
> en su templo, donde tienen
> comida y casa pagada
> todos los hombres insignes. (117)

> God shed his grace on it,
> and on me, so that I may bear it!
> For I come on behalf of Fame
> for it, because
> I wish to place it
> in her temple, where
> food and shelter are to be found
> for all famous men.

Fame as *vox populi* reinforces the idea that the gathered crowd represents the people and their admiration for the actor but at the same time there is a more exalted topological reference. Fame is said to live

> in a palace at the centre of the world, within the limits of Earth, Heaven and Sea – an echoing palace, pierced with a thousand openings, through which every voice, even the lowest, could penetrate. This palace, made entirely of bronze, was always open and every word that entered it was broadcast forth again, much amplified ... and from her palace she kept watch over the whole world. (Grimal)

The goddess of Fame, seer and hearer of all things, is understood to want the statue of Juan Rana in her palace located at the centre of the world. While this imaginary *locus* symbolizes an extraordinary site for the statue, the reference to the goddess also connects *El triunfo* with the theme of *fame*, central to *Fieras*.

Once again there is an interruption and a petition for the Juan Rana statue:

> Yo soy de las nueve hermanas
> del Parnaso mandadera,
> y me envían a buscarla,
> porque la quieren poner
> entre brujerías varias
> que hay en sus escaparates. (118)

> I am a messenger
> from the nine sisters of Parnassus,
> and they send me to fetch it,
> for they wish to place it
> among the many works of magic
> that they have on display in their halls.

Again, the mythological world of the main play is present in *El triunfo* but in this instance the symbolic reference is to the arts in general:

> It was as the god of music and poetry that Apollo was portrayed on Mount Parnassus, where he presided over the pastimes of the Muses. His oracular pronouncements were generally in the form of verse and he was thought to provide inspiration for seers as well as poets. (Grimal under Apollo)

The second demand for the Juan Rana statue can be seen as much grander than the first; it is the muses themselves and hence Apollo, the son of Zeus, who demand the Juan Rana statue at their most sacred of sites. The venerated Juan Rana, the more exemplary alter ego of Hercules, now demanded by both Fame and the muses has reached an incredible level of apotheosis. There is, however, one additional step in this process of deification, one that serves to exalt the royal family.

It is the third person who arrives demanding the Juan Rana statue that ultimately attains the privilege of possessing such an extraordinary effigy:

> SOLADO: Caballeros, el Rey manda
> que no se saque de aquí
> esta estatua de Juan Rana,
> porque quiere luego al punto

ponerla sobre la basa
de una fuente del Retiro.   (118)

SOLDIER: Gentlemen, the king commands
that this statue of Juan Rana
not be taken from this place,
for he wishes later
to place it on the base
of a fountain in the Retiro.

This statue is to be placed in the Retiro palace and used as a fountain. With the soldier attaining this privilege over the mythological gods on behalf of the king, Charles II is symbolically depicted as the most powerful of the three demanders. It is not coincidental that it is a soldier who is successful in retaining the Juan Rana statue for the king. This symbolic presence enforces the idea of a powerful king from a military standpoint. The royal victory over the gods in this theatrical scene is an unabashed bow to the royal family's superiority. Importantly, it is Juan Rana's *triunfo* that is used to applaud the royal family. Calderón's celebration of Juan Rana, the unheroic consummate fool, the alter ego of Hercules, whose statue is desired by the gods, becomes the perfect vehicle for venerating the king. Juan Rana's apotheosis is multilayered in its presentation and symbols and significantly connected to the king's desired image of supremacy. In addition to this multilayered apotheosis of Juan Rana and its veneration of the king, Calderón has woven a multilevelled presentation of reality that rivals the thought-provoking vision of reality in his *La vida es sueño.*

On one level the audience witnesses Juan Rana the actor playing his own created persona. This is a testament to the fact that the Juan Rana persona has attained such status that it exists as an entity unto itself. It is quite conceivable, therefore, that another actor could play this part. But with Juan Rana the actor playing his own independent persona, the perception of reality and the blurring of fact and fiction, of Juan Rana the actor and his persona, and of theatre and life become paramount. It must not be forgotten that Juan Rana the actor, playing his own autonomous persona, is also acting as a statue of himself. The statue represents a reproduction of his persona and as such, Juan Rana the actor is playing a sculpted double of his persona, a physical representation of his theatrical and literary double, a double of his double. This is the beginning of Calderón's ingenious, complex, and hilarious multilevelled presentation of reality.

No statue of Juan Rana ever existed but the possibility of its existence is believable considering his celebrity and the fact that another artistic representation exists of him – an anonymous portrait of the actor painted during his lifetime is now a part of the Real Academia Española's collection. The invented premise of a statue is an excellent example of the intertwining of reality and illusion – be it plausible or purely theatrical – in this *entremés* and many other Juan Rana *entremeses*. Calderón is reiterating that the invented world is at times as believable and plausible as reality itself. Our view of reality is relative, mutable, and as fragile as that presented in *La vida es sueño*. While this laudatory *entremés* moves the spectator to laughter rather than grave ponderings about life, it still embodies Calderón's moralistic and philosophical message about life, life as a dream, and our questionable perception of reality.

When Juan Rana is brought onstage on a carriage as a statue, the sculpted double of his theatrical persona, his playful reaction to this situation adds a further level to the play's questioning of reality. At the beginning, Juan Rana acts as if he does not know what is going on and as if he is 'confused' by this onstage situation: '¿Qué es esto que me pasa, santo cielo?' (115) (Dear God, what is happening to me?). He is even surprised that his statue is present: '¡Ola¡ ¿mi estatua aquí? ¡Notable caso!' (115) (Goodness! My statue here? What a strange occurrence!). The Juan Rana persona, in pretending not to realize he is playing his own statue, is trying to make us believe that he does not know he is acting. While the audience has accepted the created illusion of Juan Rana as a statue, ironically the Juan Rana persona acts as if this is not plausible to him. The persona has mockingly not partaken in the *entremes*'s presentation of reality. The audience must surely have shaken its head in disbelief and laughter at this additional level of incredible reality. Little by little, however, the Juan Rana character realizes that he is the statue, that he is playing the statue/double of himself:

De suerte que aunque había presumido
Que era yo el que venía en tanto estruendo,
Soy mi estatua, y no yo; ya lo entiendo. (114–15)

As luck would have it, though I had presumed
That I was the one arriving in such an uproar,
I am my statue, and not myself; now I understand.

While he eventually comes to realize and accept his statuesque doubling, and even comments on how well he has been assembled, Juan Rana continues to be puzzled, wondering if this perplexing event is really happening.

The Juan Rana character reflects that he surely must be at home sleeping: 'Yo apostaré que estoy ahora en mi casa/ durmiendo, sin saber lo que me pasa' (116) (I bet that right now I am at home/ sleeping, not knowing what is happening to me). Once again, Calderón makes an unequivocal reference to Segismundo's ponderings on life as a dream but here Juan Rana ironically refers to sleeping at home in a comfortable bed. Unlike Juan Rana's, Segismundo's sleeping quarters are a gloomy cavernous prison and not a cozy home. On the level of intertextuality, therefore, Juan Rana's plight can be considered a comic, carnivalesque take on Segismundo's plight in *La vida es sueño*. While Segismundo suffers a series of grave self-ponderings on the life-as-a-dream conundrum, Juan Rana's reality-bending musings are humourous in nature. In contrast to Segismundo, however, the Juan Rana character as a statue has no control over his final destination or destiny. The soldier ultimately carries him off to his final destination, atop a fountain in the Retiro.

On a more personal level, as a statue ruminating aloud on the things happening to him, it is as if Juan Rana is playing his own death; it is as if he is having an out-of-body experience. Within the confines of the play, his future is etched in stone, as it were, as compared to Segismundo who has, or so it would seem, free choice in his moral decisions. At the end of the play Escamilla's daughter appears as his soul to sing his praises and those of the royal family.

> [MANUELA]: ¡A fuera!, que el alma
> de Juan Rana soy,
> que este sayo, este cincho, esta vara
> fueron siempre el alma de su buen humor;
> y vengo veloz
> a bailar en su nombre, porque
> su efecto este día celebre major   *Repiten*
> Que alumbrando el mundo,
> viva más que el Sol
> la bella María-Ana,
> no es admiración,
> no, no, no, no, no;
> que tiene más vida
> la luz que es mayor,   *Repiten*
> no, no, no, no, no.
> Que Carlos se lleve

                    todo nuestro amor,
                    siendo Rey y hermoso,
                    no es admiración,
                    no, no, no, no, no;
                    que con tales gracias
                    hiciéralo yo,
                    no, no, no, no, no.
                    Que saquen a vista
                    de nuestro Rey [hoy]
                    al grande Juan Rana,
                    no es admiración,
                    no, no, no, no, no,
                    que como es tan Viejo
                    le sacan al Sol,
                    no, no, no, no, no.   [*Vanse*] (122)

[MANUELA]:   Away! For I am the soul
                    of Juan Rana,
                    for this tunic, this sash, this staff
                    were always the soul of his good humour;
                    and I come swiftly
                    to dance in his name, to
                    better celebrate his effect this day.   *Repeat*
                    May beautiful María-Ana,
                    lighting the world,
                    live longer than the sun,
                    it is not admiration,
                    no, no, no, no, no;
                    may the greater light
                    have longer life.   *Repeat*
                    no, no, no, no, no.
                    May Carlos have
                    all of our love,
                    being king and resplendent.
                    It is not admiration,
                    no, no, no, no, no;
                    that I might do it
                    with such grace,
                    no, no, no, no, no.
                    May they bring before

the king [today]
the great Juan Rana.
It is not admiration,
no, no, no, no, no,
for because he is so old
they bring him into the light,
no, no, no, no, no. [*Exeunt*]

We have an obvious linking between the greatness of the royal family
and that of the resplendent Juan Rana.[10] All in all, considering his death
a few months after this performance, this soulful representation by
Manuela and Juan Rana's deathlike apparition were sadly prophetic.

El triunfo continues to present an additional slant on the dream/life
theme and the perception of reality. Midway through the *entremés* when
the statue is being placed upon its fountain base in a cumbersome
fashion, Escamilla orders the statue to be quiet as if in desperation after
hearing its many asides:[11]

ESCAMILLA: ¡Calle ahí!, que las estatuas,
aunque las hagan gigote,
no pueden hablar palabra,
si no es que sea entre sí.
JUAN RANA: ¿Y aquí entre ustedes no? (119)

ESCAMILLA: Be quiet! Statues
cannot speak,
even if they are dashed to pieces,
except to themselves.
JUAN RANA: And not here amongst you people?

Escamilla and Juan Rana would seem to step out of character to speak to
each other. Within the created reality of the play, Escamilla should not
be able to hear Juan Rana's mutterings or comment on them but
Calderón has intentionally created the illusion that they break the rules
of theatre. Their short banter breaks from the reality created up to this
time and slips into another, constructing a temporal and theatrical
pause, as it were, from the *entremés* as a whole. Within the play, therefore,
there exists a hiatus, a momentary full stop in the plot of *El triunfo*. This
is metatheatrically ironic if we consider that the *entremés* itself, while
connected to the main play, is an intermissional change of theatrical

pace. This created situation remains consistent with the complex bending and blurring of reality inside and outside the play. This pause, a scripted and integral part of the *entremés*'s story line, rips away a layer of the previously established theatrical illusion to create another, but the scene still maintains its staged version of reality. It can be said that Escamilla and Juan Rana are revealing to the audience that the onstage reality is flexible and mutable. Considering the blurring of the real and the fictional inherent within the play, it is not difficult to imagine that the multilevelled presentation of reality spills over into the perceived reality of the audience. Effectively, the illusory reality-bending qualities of *El triunfo* mesh with the reality of the audience. *La vida es sueño* also played with the intertwining of what is real and what is imaginary. But while Segismundo tries to separate life from dreams and eventually comes to the conclusion that life is a dream, or at least resembles one, *El triunfo* would seem to go one step further in its metaphysical musing. The line between the onstage and the audience reality is interwoven or, in other words, the onstage blurring of fact and illusion spills over to contaminate the audience's perception of reality. In the case of *El triunfo* life is a multilevelled reality and so may be our dreamlike life.

This overlap of fact and illusion also exists in relation to the physical location of the *entremés*'s action, adding to the blurring of reality and illusion for the spectator and, above all, for the 1672 audience. Within the written text of *El triunfo*, the action takes place in an unspecified area of the *Palacio de Buen Retiro*, the royal palace, but the *entremés* was actually presented in 'El Real Coliseo de Buen Retiro' (Wilson 58), the royal theatre, situated in the very same palace. The play's locus, usually a separate onstage 'reality,' is, in this case, not separate but rather the 'true' location of the performance. The audience could easily feel that it is in a play with no separation between on- and offstage. Beyond this meshing of the locus of the *entremés* and the physical location of the theatre, the Juan Rana statue is to be placed 'sobre la basa/ de una fuente del Retiro' (118) (on the base/ of a fountain in the Retiro) in 'la Sala de las Burlas' (118) (the Hall of Practical Jokes). While no hall with this exact name exists in El Retiro, Wilson suggests that this 'Sala' refers to the *pieza de los bufones*, a room where six Velázquez portraits of court jesters were hung – a logical location to place a Juan Rana statue/ fountain (237). Fact and plausible reality are once again intertwined to form a shared space and ambiguous theatrical, physical, and metaphysical reality.

Clearly, *El triunfo de Juan Rana* is a befitting commemoration of Juan

Rana's created persona, the uniqueness of his acting, and the length of his career. By conjecture, *El triunfo* is a symbolic statue of Juan Rana sculpted in words, a monument in the Horatian sense. In relation to the present, the act of analysing *El triunfo* is in itself proof that the Juan Rana statue formed by words has survived, that the actor's fame lives. Calderón has successfully fulfilled the main goal of *El triunfo*, the apotheosis of Juan Rana. However, it would seem that Calderón, himself an aged man, is looking back on his own life and work in his celebration of the ultimate baroque actor. What this self-reflection shows us is that the playwright was able to laugh at himself and the great moralistic themes for which he is best remembered. This reveals a more light-hearted and benevolent side of his person. In writing an *entremesil* parody of *La vida es sueño*, Calderón would appear to say that life may resemble the nonsensical, multilevelled reality of dreams and that actions have some bearing on our ultimate demise but regardless, it is essential to be able to laugh at life and more precisely, at oneself. *El triunfo* represents a monument to Juan Rana, Calderón himself, and ultimately life. It is much more than a simple and straightforward celebratory tribute to Juan Rana. The goddess Fame must surely have had a hand in the writing of Calderón's *El triunfo de Juan Rana* as the memory of the life and career of this actor continues on.

If *El triunfo* interweaves the lines of on- and offstage reality, Agustín Moreto y Cavana's *Los dos Juan Ranas* (1664) keeps these two worlds separate – the spectator clearly distinguishes between reality and theatrical illusion, between stage and audience space.[12] This fundamental difference stems from the fact that *Los dos* does not concern itself with the biographical aspects of Juan Rana's life nor with the physical location of the production – the fantasy remains onstage. As such, *Los dos* represents a thematic and technical difference between the two *entremeses*. Notwithstanding, the double remains central to both, even if it takes on a different guise as a *Doppelgänger*.[13] The uncanny encounter that Juan Rana experiences with his other while physically separated from the audience does, however, hold the ability to perturb the innermost subconscious fears of the spectator.

As in the case of *El triunfo*, the beginning of *Los dos* represents an important parodic intertextual reference. Here an enamoured Juan Rana calls up from the street to the window of his beloved Bernarda as Calisto did to his Melibea in *La Celestina*.[14] As in the case of Calisto, Juan Rana is to ascend a ladder to enter Bernarda's house when her disapproving father is fast asleep. A great difference exists, however, between our protagonist and the Calisto lover. The love sonnets exchanged between Juan Rana and Bernarda are tongue-in-cheek parodies of Calisto's florid and romantic language. In opposition to the idyllically heroic Calisto and in tune with his customary characterization, Juan Rana is not only a bumbling fool but also a coward.

JUAN RANA: Bernarda hermana,
                       porque ve aqui molido de traella,
                       ya subo por ella,
                       (dexo aparte el rodar sus escalones)
                       vè aqui que alguien me vè, dize ladrones,
                       vè aqui à esta voz tu padres que despierta,
                       vè aqui la vexzidad que abre la puerta,
                       vè aqui que yo en buen duelo por tu fama,
                       antes de todo, digo que es mi dama,
                       y callar que por ti pretendo,
                       ve aqui so el Alcalde, y que me pre[n]do,
                       y ve aqui en fin, que porque mas lo notes,
                       me hago la causa, y dome cien açotes. (30)

JUAN RANA: Sister Bernarda,
                       although you see me here fatigued from carrying it [the ladder],
                       I will ascend it,
                       (I will place it here).
                       If someone sees me, they'll shout 'thief.'
                       This voice will wake your parents,
                       you'll see the vexation as the door opens,
                       you'll see that above all to save your reputation
                       I'll say that you're my lady,
                       and I will be silent.
                       I am the mayor, and if I'm taken,
                       you'll see in the end, you'll really see,
                       I'll give myself up and take my hundred lashes.

It is only through the coaxing of Bernarda, who sees his nocturnal ascension as proof of his love, that Juan Rana agrees to carry out this folly. Accordingly, Juan Rana is a comical intertexual double of Calisto, a parodic presentation of the tragic lover, and *Los dos Juan Ranas*, a comic reference to the famous tragicomedic *La Celestina*.

Unbeknown to the enraptured lovers, their nocturnal plan is over-
heard by none other than Juan Rana's jealous love rival the Sacristán
(the sexton), the soon-to-be Juan Rana *Doppelgänger*. The fact that the
rival lover is a man connected to the church, who consults 'una Vieja' for
her magical powers, represents an irreverent jab at the church for the
unchaste and unchristian behaviour of its members and yet another
intertextual reference to the famous and infamous *La Celestina*:

> [SACRISTÁN]: Remedio ay para todo.
> Aqui vive una Vieja, que de modo
> transforma las personas, que pudiera
> ser que un conjuro hiziera. (32)

> [SACRISTÁN]: There is a remedy for everything.
> An old woman lives nearby who can
> transform people; maybe
> she could cast a spell.

The old woman, much like a Celestina, performs her magic, transform-
ing the Sacristán into someone dressed exactly the same as Juan Rana. In
this way, the audience is witness to the theatrical fabrication of Juan
Rana's *Doppelgänger*. While darkness camouflages 'los dos Juan Ranas'
from initially seeing each other and allows for a comical duelling incognito dialogue, the moment of truth finally arrives – the real Juan Rana
sees his other.

The decisive visual encounter between the two Juan Ranas coincides
with what Andrew J. Webber calls the visual compulsion of the *Doppelgänger*: '(T)he autoscopic, or self-seeing, subject beholds its other self as
another, as visual object, or alternatively is beheld as object of the other
self' (3). Juan Rana experiences double vision in the *entremés* when he
finally sees his other and is understandably taken aback by this confusing
situation. When he sees his face *pintiparada* (mockingly reproduced) in
the other who dresses like him 'desde la caperuça a la polayna' (37)
(from head to toe), he wonders if indeed he himself is the other. In the
first moments of his visual trance the bewildered Juan Rana believes he is
gazing upon a mirror image that mimics his every move; in other words,
the real Juan Rana sees a doubling of himself and his actions (27). This
first reaction coincides with Sabine Melchior-Bonnet's remarks on the
mental mechanics behind the perception of our self in a mirror:

To see oneself in the mirror, to identify oneself, requires a mental operation by which the subject is capable of objectivizing himself, of separating
what is outside from what is inside. This operation can be successful if the
subject recognizes the reflection as his own likeness and can say, 'I am
the other of that other.' The relationship of self to self and the familiarity
of the self cannot be directly established and remains trapped in the reci-
procity of seeing and being seen. (5)

The appearance of his *Doppelgänger* causes an existential pondering in
the mind's eye of Juan Rana, and the protagonist, apart from experiencing self-doubt, questions his identity and the reality he thought he knew
up to this point. Juan Rana must learn to differentiate himself from the
other. Juan Rana's self-viewing coincides with Webber's explanation that
a *Doppelgänger*-induced double vision creates a 'visually compulsive
scandal' (2) within the subject and his or her perception of the world.
Sigmund Freud also discusses the feelings of dread, horror, and harbin-
ger of death that results from experiencing the uncanny and viewing
one's double (219, 235). This would describe quite accurately the scene
written for Juan Rana in *Los dos*. The famous analyst also delves into the
more deeply rooted origins of our collective fear of the uncanny:

Our analysis of instances of the uncanny has led us back to the old, animistic
conception of the universe. This was characterized by the idea that the
world was peopled with the spirits of human beings; by the subject's narcis-
sistic overvaluation of his own mental processes; by the belief in the omnipo-
tence of thoughts and the technique on that belief; by the attribution to
various outside persons and things of carefully graded magical powers,
or '*mana*'; as well as by all the other creations with the help of which man, in
the unrestricted narcissism of that stage of development, strove to fend off
the manifest prohibitions of reality. (240)

Juan Rana's encounter with his double has, therefore, the power to
reach deep into the psyche and subconscious fears of the spectator. The
Celestinesque *vieja* and her magical powers is further evidence of this
uncanny phenomenon and Juan Rana's onstage trepidation. Once again
the Juan Rana persona, as in Calderón's *El triunfo* and, indeed, in *La vida
es sueño*, questions the foundations of reality and existence.

Webber also states that the scandalous experience has in turn a divisive result on the use of language; double vision causes double-talk or, in
other words, '[the *Doppelgänger*] echoes, reiterates, distorts, parodies,

dictates, impedes, and dumbfounds the subjective faculty of free speech' (3). This speech impediment is certainly the case with the bewildered Juan Rana, forced further into a situation of 'double-talk' by the deceitful *Doppelgänger*ed Sacristán. The Sacristán asks Juan Rana, 'Eres sombra, eres fantasma,/ ilusión ò fantasia?' (36) (Are you shadow, are you phantasm,/ illusion, or fantasy?). The *Doppelgänger* who through magic has become the other turns the tables on the original, asking the original if it is not he who is the copy – quite a perplexing moment for a self-doubting original experiencing a *Doppelgänger*-induced identity crisis. The other's line of questioning unearths what can be considered a primal fear that dwells in the subconscious of the spectator when he or she hears the word 'sombra.'

In his first treatise on the *Doppelgänger*, Otto Rank speaks of the shadow from an ethnological viewpoint, highlighting its metaphoric connection to death. The biblical phrase 'in the shadow of death' makes it clear that this belief is not solely a non-Western tradition (1971, 51–2). Juan Rana's *Doppelgänger* also uses the word 'fantasma,' another word directly connected to the under/otherworld. In this way, the first two words spoken by the other Juan Rana evoke the other side of life – death. Juan Rana also wonders in this preamble whether his double vision is not a mirror image. Rank draws our attention to the Western belief that Narcissus succumbs to a self-reflective death because he is unable to separate himself from his own image reflected in a mirror like body of water (70). The mention of shadow, mirror image, and phantasm in *Los dos* gives further reason for the uncanny and primal fear felt by Juan Rana on seeing his double.[15]

After the initial arresting moments of his encounter, Juan Rana expresses his frustration with a situation that he cannot fathom:

> No hay duda, yo soy, es clara
> cosa, ò que me han resellado,
> para que vno por dos valga. (37)

> There's no doubt, 'tis I, 'tis clear,
> or they've stamped another copy of me
> so they can have two for one.

The great ability of the double/*Doppelgänger* to perplex signals one of its most important inherent and contradictory qualities. At the same time that it is used to attempt to explain the conflicting elements that exist

around us and in others – that which we push away and consider evil or
alien – it inevitably signals the otherness within us. Keppler perceptively
points out that in considering the double, '[w]hat we are to deal with ...
is the mystery of a contradiction, of simultaneous distinction and identity, of an inescapable two that are at the same time an indisputable one'
(1). Juan Rana, when confronted with his *Doppelgänger*, must contend
with an inherent duality that often remains incomprehensible, difficult
if not impossible to define because it signals the contradictory that at
times abides within ourselves:

> Que mas quiere que me vaya,
> si me vengo, y si me voy
> por dos partes tan contrarias,
> que me venida es precisa,
> y mi ida es necessaria? (37)

> How is it possible for me to leave,
> if I'm coming and going
> in two opposite directions,
> that my coming is imperative
> and my leaving is required?

Undoubtedly, the double represents the irrepressible, unwanted, contradictory, and shadowy other that is part of all of us. While this corpo-
real dualism doubtlessly gives us a base for understanding the double,
this base is limited and elementary. On the other hand, if we consider
the human psyche, with its great capacity for imagination and psychological experiences, the inherent complexity and infinite possibilities
of the double become apparent. The theatrical Juan Rana, unlike us,
however, does have the opportunity to tackle head on both the physical
and the metaphysical other.

The two Juan Ranas '*[p]onen las dos escaleras una contra otra/ y sube cada
uno por su lado*' (sd39) (place the two ladders one against the other/ and
climb up). During their parallel ascent, a physical confrontation takes
place between them causing both to fall to the ground. More grounded,
as it were, by his quick and violent descent, the real Juan Rana is knocked
to his senses, exclaiming 'este es el otro Juan Rana' (40) (that man is the
other Juan Rana). The real Juan Rana, now aware of the other as a
separate being, is forced into action when his quicker-to-the-draw
Doppelgänger unites with Bernarda on her beckoning. The jealousy felt by

the real Juan Rana now matches the initial invidious emotions of the Sacristán. The end result of this sudden physical separation and bout of jealousy is the host's resolve to become completely dissociated from his other – 'salid de los dos Juan Ranas' (41) (to emerge from the two Juan Ranas). This determination is equivalent to a death wish for the other. This wish does eventually come to fruition but not before further double trouble takes place.

In the following scene Bernarda and the other Juan Rana have now entered her house and, more precisely, her room. On her momentary and opportune exit to check on her father and to go for refreshments, Juan Rana slips into the room. After a comical scene wherein the *Doppelgänger* does not share his food and drink with the gluttonous Juan Rana, the double trouble finale occurs. With the father's awakening and bombastic entrance into his daughter's room both Juan Ranas are trapped together – a befitting situation for a dual face-off. The real Juan Rana is almost undone by his rival whose double-talk is far superior to his own – the spell-bound double almost convinces the witnesses who have arrived that he is the real Juan Rana. However, the real Juan Rana is saved when a deus ex machina neighbour who has seen all reveals the true identity of the impostor, the jealous and conniving Sacristán.

Juan Rana's portrayal of this uncanny encounter with his *Doppelgänger* and its final 'all's well that ends well' resolution is in tune with his usual bumbling underdog characterization in many *entremeses*. The use of the *Doppelgänger* with its compulsively visual component and ensuing scandal evoked double-talk also befits the performative Juan Rana persona. The intertexual references to *La Celestina* add a parodic subtext to an *entremés* already rich in situational comedy. However, while the menacing evil of the *Doppelgänger* is gleefully overcome in *Los dos Juan Ranas*, 'the shadow and mirror-image of death' cannot be overlooked as a subconscious presence in the spectator. It must also be remembered that the inter-texually evoked Calisto did not experience such a happy ending as our carnivalesque protagonist – this is yet another reference to death. While Juan Rana is histrionically scared out of his wits, facing his darker side, the play-goer hysterically laughs at his or her own mirror image of death, albeit subconsciously. Consequently, the spectator is laughing in the face of death while laughing at Juan Rana's seemingly innocent *Doppelgänger* predicament. In the end, the intertextual and parodic *Los dos Juan Ranas* furnishes us with an ingenious use of the theatrical *Doppelgänger*, ambiguous in its parodic dance-of-death evocation.

In Gerónimo de Cáncer y Velasco's *Juan Ranilla* the evil other/

Doppelgänger is once again a central motif, but here the menacing other, as the title suggests, is a miniature Juan Rana.[16] In this case, size is not important as this wee one wages much havoc in the life of his grand originator. This Juan Ranilla represents the resentful and conniving alter ego of the happy-go-lucky rural mayor, who is much like the Sacristán Juan Rana in *Los dos*. Here, however, it is not jealousy that drives the other to compete with Juan Rana but rather a question of power. Curiously, in this instance Juan Rana plays second fiddle to his double – it is the double who dominates the stage and moves the plot forward. In many ways, therefore, *Juan Ranilla* is a parodic take on the Juan Rana trademark – the bumbling country mayor.

Juan Rana was so successful at the mayor mask he created that, while many attempts were made after his death, no other actor was ever to make this role come alive. *Juan Ranilla* is an excellent example of how the well-known Juan Rana mask has taken on a life of its own, engendering spin-offs from an invented theatrical figure. In this instance the mini-Juan Rana *Doppelgänger* is a negative force that greatly resents his namesake, feels belittled due to his dependence on Juan Rana for his existence, and fiercely detests being merely a mayor 'de minotivo' – which in itself is quite comical, as the original Juan Rana is already a stubby fellow.

As an antagonistic alter ego, Juan Ranilla swears to avenge the one who makes him feel small:

RANILLA: He Dios que si consigo deste modo
           el verme dèl vengado,
           que ha de saber la villa,
           qual el Juan Rana es,
           qual el Juan Ranilla. (213)

RANILLA: By God, if I manage to
           revenge myself upon him,
           the whole city will know
           which is Juan Rana
           and which Juan Ranilla.

Indeed, the evil alter ego plots to eliminate his alter ego and to rid himself of Juan Rana; Juan Ranilla stages a criminal trick. Juan Rana is set up to be falsely accused of murder, a sombre and threatening situation much like that of the bedevilled Juan Rana in *Los dos Juan Ranas*.

After the fabricated crime is successfully carried out, the victimized Juan Rana is dragged off to prison, unable to prove his innocence. Even the miraculous jailhouse apparition of his presumed victim in the guise of a famished 'combidado de piedra' (stone guest) does not make the gullible Juan Rana suspicious that he has been tricked.[17] In this way the manipulative Ranilla alter ego would seem to be ultimately victorious over his unsuspecting and simple namesake:

> RANILLA: Vè como es un tonto; señor Juan Rana
>   Y que Juan Ranilla lleva la gala? (224)

> RANILLA: See how stupid he is; Mr Juan Rana
>   And that Juan Ranilla is winning the day?

It would seem that the smaller alter ego will be successful in stamping out his defining father.

From a Freudian perspective, this Juan Ranilla represents the super ego unable to repress his Oedipal impulses, and in this sense the belittled Ranilla attempts to eliminate the parental figure. In doing so, he is trying to set himself free from his defining counterpart whose mere existence places him in an inferior position. This grotesque parody of Oedipus must have been quite effective, considering that Juan Rana, as can be seen in his portraits, is already quite short and stout. What we have, therefore, is a parody of the already parodied real life 'other.'

The resentment and hate felt towards the grander Juan Rana by his smaller counterpart also leads the analysis to another *Doppelgänger* premise indicated by Webber. He points out that there is often a power play between ego and alter ego (4). The resentment of Juan Ranilla, therefore, represents his frustration and rebellion against tutelage, surrogacy, and subordination to his 'master' (4). Here, however, there is an inversion of the host/ego and double/alter ego relationship – it is the double that wishes to kill off his host rather than the other way around. Within the thematic bounds of this *entremés* it is important to note that this wishful killing of Juan Rana by his alter ego has significant psychoanalytical implications. With the hypothetical killing of Juan Rana, Juan Ranilla would cease to have an identity or a reason for being. Juan Ranilla's existence is dependent on the existence of Juan Rana whether he likes it or not – the miniature other can only be defined in relation to what he is compared to, as the negative of the positive, as the other of the original. Consequently, if this *Doppelgänger* should be successful in killing his father, he will be successful at killing himself. Oddly enough, therefore, the Juan Ranilla *Doppelgänger* allows for the strange and enigmatic situation of a patricide/suicide. It is fitting, therefore, that the open-ended *Juan Ranilla* leaves the audience dangling as to the fate of Juan Rana/Juan Ranilla.

Another Juan Ranilla *Doppelgänger* very different from the 'de minotivo' mayor of *Juan Ranilla* makes an appearance in *El retrato de Juan Rana* (Villaviciosa).[18] The portrait noted in the title is the chief theatrical motif and motor of this *entremés*. While surely an allusion to the existing Juan Rana portrait, the *entremés* as a whole questions the discipline itself and the selective reality that it represents. The portrait is, of course, a venerated and highly symbolic genre that involves a unique relationship between the artist and the painted subject, especially if that person is of great social and political stature. Sebastián Covarrubias Orozo's 1611 definition of *retrato* refers to '(l)a figura contrahecha de alguna persona principal y de cuenta, cuya efigie y semejanza es justo quede por memoria a los siglos venideros' (the reproduced likeness of a well-known and well-regarded important person, whose effigy and semblance are worthy of being remembered for centuries to come). The moral and social restriction of portrait subjects so clearly noted in Covarrubias's definition would seem unique in early European dictionaries (Pommier 288–9). In early seventeenth-century Spain, therefore, the portrait is specifically defined as a sacrosanct site for those of power seen worthy of remembrance and example. Portraiture has been used for centuries as a tool to project a particular image, a manufactured representation that the sitter wishes to be seen by his or her subjects, and that the ultimately wishes to live on after his death. Used as a tool for self-promotion, fame, and wishful immortality, the portrait has much in common with theatre itself. Ernst Robert Curtius specifically notes this important link within a Spanish context:

> The close companionship of the arts, especially of dramatic poetry and painting, is of course not based only upon the Christian world picture of the Spanish period of florescence but also upon the pomp and display of the monarchy. Charles V and Phillip II were art lovers and collectors of pictures. The imperial splendor of these rulers, whose taste remained authoritative both for the nobility and for their feeble successors, gave painting, and particularly the art of portraiture, that rank in practice which the theoretical deductions of scholars contemporaneously attested. (569)

The portrait with its theatrical representation of power was obviously well understood and employed by the Spanish royal family of the day.

This 'means to an end' usage of the portrait by those in power forces us to question the reality represented within the portrait's frame especially in light of Curtius's mention of the successive weak Spanish rulers. How true or illusory is the reality represented in portraits exalting the leaders of Spain in this period? Where does reality end and illusion begin? Ultimately, the royal portrait and that of other influential subjects must be considered a fabricated version of reality, a mixture of veracity and self-serving illusion, an idealized view of the subject. Once again these questions of representation show great links between the portrait and the theatre and a staged representation of reality. *El retrato* exposes this selective and deceptive view of the subject and reality, while representing the evolution of the portrait as a genre.

Significantly, the definition of *retrato* in the Real Academica Española's *Diccionario de la Lengua Española*, published in the mid-eighteenth century, has excluded Covarrubias's moral and social restrictions altogether. This significant change infers that the idea of the portrait was in flux and evolving from its restrictive interpretation to a broader interpretation of the genre. Covarrubias's historical definition of the portrait remains a significant indicator of the restrictive, idealized, and socially conservative starting point from which the concept of the portrait is based in this period. This evolution of the portrait is noted by Vicente Carducho in 1632 when he complains in *Dialogos de la pintura* of the proliferation of the portrait and its vulgarization. He speaks of portraits of ordinary men and women posing in a manner that should only be reserved for royalty and those of noble standing (Pommier 228). The writer's dismay for what he sees as the denigration of the portrait is proof of the evolution of the genre; it is no longer just a tool for self-promotion of the most powerful. Max J. Friedländer explains that in the case of Velázquez the difference between the artist's royal portraits and those of less noble birth is quite significant:

To begin with, the high-rankers were far from patient models. Then the favourite, who was nevertheless a subject, was forbidden any penetrating observation, all impartial impressions when face to face with his King. And lastly Majesty, to portray which was his primary duty, could more easily be rendered visible by costume, insignia, princely occupation like hunting or the equestrian art, than in the face, especially as at the time of the painter the thin-blooded and worn-out Spanish Royal House lacked any forceful-looking ruler and individuality was strangulated by ceremonial. The Master's spiritual freedom excelled most of all when he was with men who were socially inferior to him, describing the comical existence of the Court jesters and dwarfs with telling sureness. (251)

It would seem, therefore, that painting the king and other nobles was at times an onerous task and that the royal sitter restricted and limited the painter's artistic freedom. Surely, the portrait itself had to become more deceptive in its depiction of reality if we consider the progressively debilitated royal sitters. While perhaps the great Velázquez was less restrained and controlled than most portraitists, some limiting of artistic freedom is inherent due to the sitter's rank and the painterly restrictions that the genre demanded. It was ultimately the sitter, however, who controlled the final product:

> Apart from the fact that the object, the appearance given, demands to be observed accurately and objectively, thus limiting the artist's freedom, his imagination, his spirit, the portraitist is quite specifically in a subservient position to the patron – who even if he does not consider himself knowledgeable in matters of art, still thinks he knows himself better than the artist and therefore feels entitled to pronounce judgment on the portraitist's performance. (232)

The power was in the hands of the patron. While Velázquez's portraits of buffoons and court jesters were commissioned by the royal family and 'served to accentuate by way of contrast the majesty of the royal figures they accompanied either side by side on the canvas or with the space of palace halls' (Bass 3), they nonetheless were sites of more artistic freedom. It is the painter who has the freedom to depict as he wishes without the controlling and powerful gaze of an influential sitter. The power in the portraits of those of lesser birth is in the hands of the painter and not the sitter. The sitter's lower social status frees the artist and allows him to depict reality with fewer imposed restrictions. *El retrato* refers to the existing Juan Rana portrait à la Velázquez, and the artistic freedom of this other type of representation allows for a commentary on the issues of power inherent to the genre and to society.

In *El retrato*, the portrait appears as a mini-*Doppelgänger*, a helpless orphan girl who appears only at the end of the *entremés*. She is not an independence-seeking adult wishing to commit patricide, as in the case of the earlier Juan Ranilla, but rather a child looking for a father; she is looking for the protection that comes with dependence. However, the needy abandoned child is but an onstage fabrication by Juan Rana's scheming wife who wants to keep him under her control under the pretence of protecting him. *El retrato* is not only a perfect example of the misogynist *topos* of the controlling strong wife and her counterpart, the weakly henpecked husband,[19] but also a false 'self-reflection' of our protagonist. Importantly, the dynamics of the portrait in this *entremés* combine, in an inverted matter, the issues of power and control intrinsic to the portrait.

In the preplay action, Juan Rana has announced his intention to go to the royal court so as to make better use of his talents (52). This allusion to the royal court is important when combined with the portrait. It is not a surprising scenario that prior to Juan Rana's appearance, his wife Casilda laments the 'simplicidades' of her husband, the bumbling mayor. She fears that her 'jumento' (ass) of a husband will be taken advantage of by the court-wise ruffians, a not too unimaginable plight. With the help of her cohorts she develops a plan to stop her husband's departure. After some initial stalling, the painterly *burla* (practical joke) that will inevitably keep Juan Rana in his place occurs.

Juan Rana is asked to sit for a portrait under the pretence that his constituents need a visual reminder of him to console themselves in his absence. This is the deceptive ruse invented by his wife. Juan Rana as a fidgety and difficult sitter is reminiscent of the impatient royal poser. As mayor, he is, of course, a less imposing power figure but nonetheless a mocking royal reference is easily imagined. Juan Rana is finally shown his portrait but the image is not a painted portrait but rather is a young girl dressed up like Juan Rana posing within a frame – a real '*retrato en vivo*' (tableau) as it were. This is truly deceptive representation taken to the extreme. With the young female Juan Ranilla posing as his painted image and the others joining in on the illusion, we have metatheatrical performance where the joke is obviously on Juan Rana. As Barry Saunders has explained, the audience takes great pleasure in laughing at the expense of another because somehow it makes them feel better and better off. What the spectator is comically witnessing is an ingenious commentary on the issue of power and how it is used in society.

Although initially taken aback by this miraculous rendering, the gullible Juan Rana eventually is much taken with his 'reproduction' and is emotionally swayed by the young female Juan Ranilla's story. Juan Ranilla, played by the daughter of the same Escamilla of *El triunfo*, speaks of being an orphan and calls on the Christian virtues of the protagonist to not 'dexar desamparado/ a un retrato tan niño' (57) (leave unprotected/ such a young portrait). Juan Rana is moved to tears and promises not to abandon his smaller likeness. This physical appearance of another Juan Ranilla is indeed a double vision but it is nonetheless a very different case from the evil *Doppelgängers* previously seen in *Los dos* and in *Juan Ranilla*. On a symbolic level, however, the Juan Rana persona is 'reborn' onstage in the guise of an orphan child who is readily adopted by the sentimental mayor.[20] This Juan Ranilla is a *Doppelgänger* of the protagonist and as such is a projection of his ego – from a Freudian perspective, Juan Ranilla is a reproduction of the protagonist. In the same vein, Juan Rana's unsuccessful flight from his home life as a henpecked husband is a failed attempt to free himself from the supervision of his controlling wife. Fooled into staying, the Juan Rana ego is stifled or, in other words, the development of his ego is arrested. He remains under the control of his supervising and protective wife and cannot go out into the world. Paradoxically, however, it is the acceptance of paternal responsibility that holds him back – the thwarted Juan Rana chooses to be a protector in his own right. Juan Rana's protective instincts, in contrast to those of his wife, would seem more positive and genuine in their make-up. He wishes to protect and be a parent, as opposed to his wife who wishes to control and arrest his self-development. Juan Rana, therefore, is on one level a controlled, henpecked and childlike husband while on the other a protective and loving adoptive father, albeit of a false orphan.

This visual fabrication, part of a long *engaño de los ojos* (looks can be deceiving) tradition and the tradition of the portrait, shows that Juan Rana's wife and her cohorts have triumphed in deceiving him.[21] In comparison to the royal portrait, there is a significant change in the distribution of power. Here it is the sitter who is fooled into believing in his own representation and not those who look upon it. In contrast to the courtly portrait where the painter is subservient to the sitter, it is the sitter who is subservient not to the painter but to those who invented the ruse. This use of the portrait by Villaviciosa effectively exposes its innate power to deceive, to manipulate, and to gain control over others but here the tables are turned on the person who holds power. *El retrato* in revealing the innate deceptiveness of the portrait ultimately shows that all representation holds the potential for misrepresentation. Underlying this message is a grand social and political comment that those who hold positions of power and are accustomed to wielding it can easily be tricked into losing their authority.

In Moreto y Cavana's *La loa de Juan Rana* a framed optical illusion is also employed to trick our ingenuous protagonist into believing what others want him to see and ultimately, into doing what they want him to do.[22] While in *El retrato* Juan Rana is tricked into believing he is seeing a portrait come alive in the female Juan Ranilla, in *La loa* he is tricked into believing that his changing mirror image is the reflection of his great acting and transformist abilities. In this work the mirror has a practical function related to the introductory nature of the *loa* but this reflective theatrical prop is also a potent symbol imbued with historical, social, moral, and philosophical meaning.

From a structural point of view, it must be remembered that a *loa* is the interlude to be performed prior to the first act of the main play. Emilio Cotarelo y Mori explains that

(t)an natural obvio parece, que al comenzar la representación de una pieza cualquiera, se advierta á los espectadores lo que van á oir, que esta clase de introducciones se hallan en todos los teatros antiguos y modernos, bien que su denominación sea muy distinta. (vi–vii)

it seems so obvious and natural, that at the beginning of a production of any play, the spectators should be told about what they are going to hear, that this type of introduction is found in all ancient and modern theatres, even though it may be called something very different.

As such it is an extremely important part of the theatrical production as a whole, as it must create the necessary ambience for the entire theatre production and predispose the minds of the spectators to enter into the desirable mindset of theatrical illusion. In *La loa* the intertwining of reality and illusion is as central as it is in *El triunfo*. In the case of *El triunfo*, it is the actor's life that serves as the basis for the *entremés*'s real and illusory intertwining, and independent from the *entremés*'s story line is the fact that Juan Rana was actually petitioned back from retirement by the royal family to perform. With *La loa*, however, the premise is an order by the royal family that he perform at the Palacio; the situation that served as historical background in *El triunfo* is the main storyline for *La loa*. Consequently, the authenticity of the royal petition and the onstage enactment of it cause reality and plausible illusion to become intertwined once again. *La loa de Juan Rana* fulfils its purpose as a scintillating opening act that creates an intriguing point of departure for the afternoon's royal entertainment. The use of the mirror itself also alludes to the court, as we shall see.

While various implements have been used over the centuries by many cultures for gazing at oneself, it is in the fifteenth century that the Venetians made great advances in glass and mirror technology (MacFarlane 70). The mirror was not, however, an object of widespread use and remained a luxury article coveted by the rich and powerful in the later part of the seventeenth century (Melchior-Bonnet 27). The appearance of the mirror in *La loa* refers, therefore, to an item out of reach of most of the audience, a status symbol connected to the court and those who frequented it. Apart from this historical referencing there are many other connections to courtly life and the social condition in this *entremés*.

The opening monologue by Juan Rana is quite significant for this *loa* and for the Juan Rana persona in general. He alludes to his well-known arrest for *el pecado nefando* in 1636, stating that he does not care any more about the whole incident nor does anyone fault him or gossip about it: '¡Alabado sea Dios, santo y bendito!/ De todo el mundo no se me da un pito./ Ya denguno haze burla de mis menguas,/ y ya no me mermuran malas llenguas' (431) (Praise be to God, holy and blessed! Nobody gives a damn/ Nobody makes fun of my shortcomings/ and the evil tongues have stopped wagging). The key word here is *mengua*, or that which is lacking from something for it to be whole. Equally, it means an offence which causes one's honour to be less than whole. While these two definitions refer to what can be considered character faults, there is also an important reference to the question of honour. The most dishonourable incident in Juan Rana's life is undoubtedly his arrest for the *pecado nefando*. The opening monologue is based on a past event of the offstage Juan Rana's life and his reflection upon it but, of course, a grain of truth does not eliminate the ever-present possibility for fictionalization.

As the result of his public arrest, the onstage Juan Rana declares that he is no longer easily fooled. In a broader sense he tells us that one can never be too disbelieving: 'Ya nada me hazen creer con desemulo,/ ¡no ay vida como ser muy incredulo!/ A nadie he de creer mucho, ni poco' (431) (I'm not gullible anymore/ there's nothing like being mistrustful! / I don't trust anyone at all, not even a little). While these lines refer directly to his past experience, they are also meant as words of wisdom for the audience – as theatre *aficionados* and human beings one must be leery of what one sees. As in the earlier lines of this monologue, the final lines refer to the act itself of believing, an essential part of any successful theatre production: 'Ni a mí me he de creer, si no me toco./ ¿Si estoy aquí? Lo dudo ciertamente' (431) (I don't even believe in my existence, if I don't pinch myself./ Am I here? I highly doubt it). He is, therefore, musing on his own inability to believe even his own thoughts and existence. Juan Rana is saying that seeing is not believing. This self-doubting on the part of Juan Rana plants a seed of self-questioning in the mind of the spectator vis-à-vis his or her own viewing of reality and existence. From the onset, therefore, this *loa* embodies a reflection of the inherent ambiguities of theatre and, indeed, life. These opening reflections are in tune with centuries of thought on the mirror and its inherent and complex properties:

> The questions asked of the mirror varied throughout the centuries. The mode of knowing depended on the status bestowed on the reflection: icon, imitation, or sign. The field of subjectivity – knowledge and self-conscious-ness – slowly extricated itself from the religious perspective that created and shaped it, and at the same time, the mastery of reflection and perspective conferred a new power upon man – the power to manipulate his image, to distort it regardless of the divine resemblance contained in it. (Melchior-Bonnet 131).

Juan Rana's short monologue in its setup for the rest of the *loa* is supersaturated with references to centuries of thought on the mirror and its power to reflect the human condition. Once again, reflection is the optimal word for this *loa*.

Within the main action of this *loa*, Orozco, the bearer of the royal petition, finds Juan Rana unwilling to go to the Palacio. Juan Rana, having set the scene, now goes into character. Orozco is quite surprised at this turn of events as '[s]iempre a Palacio oced alegremente/ solía ir' (432) (you were always quite willing to go to the Palacio). Juan Rana refuses to go, as he considers himself a changed man. Indeed, in the opening five pages of this *entremés*, he exaggeratedly repeats not once but eight times, 'pues ya estò muy deferente' (I am now very different). This repetition in itself makes the audience sceptical that a true change has taken place. With regard to the petition, Juan Rana goes so far as to question: 'No ay quien haga estos papeles,/ ¿qué puedo hazer yo?' (433) (Isn't there anyone else who can play these parts?/ what can I do?). Orozco's simple reply is quite significant: 'Juan Rana, sois muy general' (433) (Juan Rana, you are a man of many talents). This remark on an initial and nonironic level refers to the straightforward meaning of *general*, a person who has knowledge of a broad range of arts and sciences. Juan Rana in this sense is qualified as a talented actor whose knowledge of his art is great. This well-known fact refers to Juan Rana the person and not the bumbling persona. In using flattery, Orozco plays on Juan Rana's vanity and pride. The soon-to-appear mirror is of course the quintessential site for discussion of these weaknesses:

> The mirror became part of the religious vocabulary of the Middle Ages, which developed its symbolic meanings from scriptural writings, Neoplatonic texts, and the patristic tradition. The utilitarian and self-reflexive use of the object is more or less ignored by these texts, as it also was in medieval iconography, both which envisaged the mirror image as either 'an idealized vision or a pejorative projection,' either a reflection of God or an instrument of the devil. (Melchior-Bonnet 108)

Juan Rana's reply sets the stage, however, for considering other meanings of *general*, with an ambiguity that reflects the ambiguity found in the opening monologue and its central message. In his reply to Orozco Juan Rana gives one meaning of *general*: 'Él miente,/ que ni cabo esquadra soy' (433) (He lies,/ I am not the head of a squadron). With his characteristic maladroit language use and misunderstanding of meaning, Juan Rana has interpreted *general* to mean the head of an armed force. This is quite obviously a misinterpretation of the context by our protagonist, but this in-character act hints at the duplicitous nature of this word and of language itself. Another meaning is given by Covarrubias: that which is common and ordinary and not learned. This fits Juan Rana's persona, the simple-minded and uneducated buffoon. It could also be interpreted to mean common property. In this sense, Juan Rana's persona embodies the common and universal faults of everyone – he as a *gracioso* is a *pharmakos* for the general faults of human nature and baroque society. This interpretation is also valid if we consider the general role of the *gracioso* and that of Juan Rana in particular. The *gracioso* embodies the other within us and in society as a whole, that which is considered bad or odd, dull-witted and awkward, that which we try to pass off as part of another entity. This is perfectly in tune with René Girard's ideas on the actor as scapegoat for the ills of society.

Of course, without Juan Rana's initial misinterpretation of *general* it would be pure conjecture to consider double meanings in this case. However, his dubious understanding of *general* opens the door for other meanings and highlights the fact that many possible interpretations of this word exist. In this way, one word with its various meanings has clearly underlined the ambiguity of language. Consequently, while Juan Rana has openly stated in his monologue that seeing is not believing, his misuse and misunderstanding of language also show that hearing is not believing, that the interpretive process of language can potentially lead to ambiguity. This misuse and misunderstanding is also a very important part of Juan Rana's success as a bumbling country bumpkin. The important and questionable nature of meaning is ever-present in the Juan Rana *entremeses* and coincides, as in this *loa*, with the ambiguity of Juan Rana's persona. The spectator is continuously befuddled by Juan Rana's duplicitous identity as he or she is by double meanings. Truths about his life are continuously mixed with the fabrications of his widely revered persona.

In this same interpretive vein, Orozco once again makes reference to Juan Rana's career and past in an attempt to make Juan Rana listen to reason:

> ¿No sois vos
> quien creistéis de repente
> ser volatin, y que andando
> por suelo llano, como éste,
> andavais por la maroma? (433)

> Isn't it you
> who suddenly thought
> you were a funambulist, and that walking
> on solid ground, like this,
> you were walking on a wire?

While a *maroma* is literally a cable or a thick rope, there is also a figurative meaning for 'andar en la maroma' (walking on a tightrope):

> Phrase, con que además del sentido recto, se da à entender que alguna persona esta incluida en algun negocio peligroso, y de dificultosa compostúra. Díxose à semejanza del volàtin, que anda por ella con sumo riesgo. (*Diccionario de Autoridades*)

> Phrase which, apart from its literal meaning, implies that a person is involved in a dangerous and difficult affair, a situation which resembles that of the funambulist, who incurs great risk when walking on the tightrope.

Orozco's words match the figurative definition of *maroma* and in doing so refer on one level to Juan Rana's past theatrical roles where the fine

line between success and failure is dependent on the actor's interpretation of the role. At the same time, however, his *pecado nefando* past, well
known to the audience of this era and highlighted in his opening
monologue, is most definitely a 'negocio peligroso.'

Considering the imperative nature of his visit and the out-of-sorts state
of Juan Rana, Orozco must find some ingenious way to convince Juan
Rana that he is the only one who can perform this six-character, one-
actor *loa*. Orozco's means of tricking the gullible Juan Rana ties together
the different 'self-reflection' levels of this *entremés*. Up to this point in the
entremés we have discussed the mental 'self-reflective' nature of *La loa*.
We have considered Juan Rana's self-pondering words of wisdom, the
self-reflective nature of theatre and in a more global sense the
(mis)perception of life and reality. From these mental levels of interpretation, we move to a more visual meaning of this term – the reflection
seen in a mirror. This self-reflection is Orozco's 'magical' mirror in
which Juan Rana believes he sees himself as the six different characters
of *La loa*.[23] The protagonist 'sees' himself transformed with this special
mirror into many *tipos*. First he becomes the *gracioso* Escamilla, then 'el
galan de la loa,/ la flor de Olmedo' (437)[24] (the hero of the loa,/ the
flower of Olmedo), and finally the *viejo* Godoy (437–8). These roles
represent the typical male cast of an *entremés* – *gracioso* (buffoon), *galán*
(gallant), and *viejo* (graybeard). The other roles that Juan Rana reflects
upon are those of María de Quiñones and María de Prado, two of the
most famous actresses of this period (438–40). Also, in the final lines of
the *entremés* Juan Rana says, 'A la Escamilla imita/ Rana en los tonos'
(440) or, in other words, he imitates the singing of the *graciosa* (the
female buffoon). Thus, Juan Rana believes that he has been converted
into all of the members, male and female, of the *loa*'s cast within the
framed mirror, but this is, of course, an illusory trick that only he does
not see through. This succession of mirrored appearances and Juan
Rana's personal identification with them is not unlike the 'mirror stage'
as described by Lacan (2–6). Juan Rana has been transformed from what
can be seen as a grumpy childlike diva into a man who accepts his place
in life, albeit through trickery.

The later section of *La loa* is actually a metatheatrical performance as
was the case in *El retrato*. Here, however, the metaperformance is made
evident by the stage instructions: '*Vanse, y salen los musicos, y a media copla
que canten salen Rana y Orozco por otra parte*' (sd 433) (Exeunt, and enter
musicians, and in mid-verse enter Rana and Orozco from the other
side). The musicians also announce the start of the *loa* as if it were a
busker show:

Vengan a vèr la loa,
que haze Juan Rana,
que es de seis personas,
y èl solo es tantas.
Vengan a vèr la loa,
que haze seis personas
una persona. (435)

Come and see the *loa*
that Juan Rana is performing,
that's a six-man show,
and he does it all.
Come and see the loa
where one person
plays six.

In this sense, within *La loa* itself, there have been two preambles to a metatheatrical production: the first, Juan Rana's monologue, and the second, the exchange between Juan Rana and Orozco. Significantly, *La loa*, which physically frames and sets up the main production, encases three sections. Added to this framed effect is, of course, the main vehicle of creating illusion – a framed mirror. Unequivocally, the multiple framing effect of this *entremés* parallels the mirror trick played on Juan Rana that makes him believe Orozco. In other words, the multi-framed structure of *La loa* is similar to the multiframed mirror illusion of the metatheatrical production. This metatheatrical production truly mirrors the spectator experiencing theatre – we are watching a reflection of the theatre experience itself.

Considering the presentation of the protagonist as a whole, it is as if there were two different Juan Ranas in this *loa*. The first Juan Rana is the monologist who expounds on his acting and personal experiences and the wisdom learned from them, speaking directly to the audience. This Juan Rana actually sets up the main body of the *loa* by stating, albeit ironically, its message: do not believe everything that you see. This message is grounded in factual information from his own life and, importantly, this Juan Rana alludes to what must have been the most painful experience of his life, his arrest for the *pecado nefando*. Therefore, we first receive Juan Rana's tongue-in-cheek warning words in the monologue and learn his lesson of 'seeing is not believing' by his negative example. The first Juan Rana is a reflection of the real actor's life and, indeed, presents a philosophical examination of it. In this sense we are truly set up by the first Juan Rana at the beginning of the *loa* into experiencing its main message. The audience's theatrical experience parallels Orozco's setting up of the second Juan Rana in the body of the work.

The second Juan Rana is, of course, the archetypal one, the persona who repeatedly says he is different in this *loa* but who, as we learn, has not changed at all. This is the gullible and simple *gracioso* so well known and loved by his contemporaries. Regardless of what the first Juan Rana says in his monologue, the second is tricked and outwitted by Orozco's fabricated mirror images – Juan Rana finally agrees to go to the Palacio.

There is much irony in the conception of *La loa* as a whole. First, the driving force behind *La loa* is a fantastical upcoming *loa* production at the Palacio where Juan Rana must be persuaded to be the principal *gracioso*. In reality, of course, this is already taking place before our eyes. *La loa* was written for and performed at the Palacio as the title page of the first edition attests (Wilson 56), and as such is an autoreferential reflection on the theme of self-reflection each time it is read or performed. It is a mind-boggling weave of meta-self-reflection and production. Symbolically it is as if two mirrors, one representing the onstage and the other the offstage audience, are facing each other, reflecting what they see on a physical and metaphysical level. The most extraordinary facet of this theatrical self-reflection is that the mirror itself is an illusion. But what is the reflection or image we see in the mirror but the inversion or opposite of what we really are? In other words, the image we hold of ourselves is not a true one, like the multiple images that Juan Rana believes are himself. We, like Juan Rana, are part of this particular 'mirror stage.'

On the whole, *La loa* is an ingenious means to highlight the troupe's famed star performer and to introduce the whole cast of the upcoming *entremeses*. It is also a fine example of the Juan Rana doubling effect – in this *loa* the audience witnesses not one but six Juan Rana doublings, both male and female, a gender-bending aspect of the mask, which will be discussed in chapter 3. Consequently, *La loa* – like *El triunfo* – is laudatory in nature and uses the double as its main rhetorical figure, but here, however, the doubling is amazingly multiple. The mirrored illusion used to trick the gullible Juan Rana into believing that he is the only one who can rise to the challenge of the *loa* and its demanding roles makes the spectators feel that he or she is in on a joke. This staged complicity makes the spectators believe that they are united with the stage actors, that they are in on the action, that they along with the other actors are pulling a fast one on Juan Rana – the audience is made to believe that it is only Juan Rana who does not see through the mirror illusion. While Lope de Vega in *El arte nuevo de hacer comedias* rightly states that 'el hablar equívoco ha tenido ... gran lugar en el vulgo,' (equivocal speech is greatly enjoyed ... by the masses), as this case shows, *el ver equívoco* (equivocal seeing) could easily be added to the equation (212).[25]

While *La loa de Juan Rana* with its theatrically framed mirror image is the most overt reference to the self-reflective Juan Rana double/ *Doppelgänger*, all of the *entremeses* analysed in this chapter are in their own way a reflection, if not a reproduction, of our protagonist. A confused statue, a magically transformed jealous rival, a resentful minimayor, a henpecked husband as a live portrait, and a host of mirror images; all represent a reflection of the original Juan Rana. While small biographical truths about the original Juan Rana would appear to crop up in many of these *entremeses*, the cross-over between fact and illusion is so great as to create confusion – a desirable characteristic for the dubious double. As such, Juan Rana is continuously double acting in the onstage and offstage world created for him by circumstance and the many *entremesistas* and producers wishing to profit from his doubleness. Juan Rana's need to appear ambiguous as an actor and a person gave double meaning to everything he played in and as. It was as if he himself were a double being living a double life – not a far-fetched idea for a gay man in this or any era. Ultimately, the self-reflective Juan Rana, whose performances and life were replete with meaningful ambiguity, creates occasion for self-reflection in the mind of the play-goer.

3 Crossing the Gendered 'Clothes'-Line[1]

The multiple and multifaceted doublings of the Juan Rana persona created by various playwrights generated an ambiguous and evocative stage representation of identity. This staged persona based in part on the actor's well-known person showed identity to be mutable, undefinable, and illusory. The end result of this perplexing presentation of identity was an onstage metaphysical questioning of reality itself which undoubtedly caused self-doubt and self-reflection in the minds of some spectators, be it on a conscious or subconscious level. As such, the playwrights who wrote for Juan Rana and the actor himself showed that the perception of identity and reality lies in a state of ever-changing flux, in a position of undefinable in-betweenness. Juan Rana's well-known homosexuality was used to fashion yet another perception of in-betweenness that put into question the most basic foundation of patriarchal society, the male/female binary classification. In this case, the highly symbolic use of clothes serves to blur and challenge societally constructed ideas on fixed sex and gender identity that are still in question today.

On a purely utilitarian level, clothes are worn to guard the body against the natural elements. They also serve to hide one's private person and thus shield it from the unwanted gaze of others. As a protective outer layer, clothes can be called our second skin, but obviously this second skin cannot be considered as merely a shielding safeguard against nature. Clothes in their 'fashion' have come to symbolize and mean much about a person and the society in which that individual lives. This 'put on' second skin is a public and symbolic display of our station in life, our sex, and our gender that in most cases is constructed and enforced by tradition and society. If today the relative social and economic mobility we enjoy is reflected in our relaxed attitude towards dress codes, the socioeconomic immutability of seventeenth-century Europe is mirrored in the nearly impossible shedding of one's second skin. Notwithstanding, fissures began to appear in the shielding and controlling second skin of baroque Spain.

While our 'dressed-down' approach to clothes would seem to signify a more egalitarian society today, there remains, however, one highly stigmatized and time-honoured 'infraction' of the gendered dress code, cross-dressing. In the most general sense, '[d]ress traditionally has been a ubiquitous symbol of sexual differences, emphasizing social conceptions of masculinity and femininity. Cross dressing, therefore, represents a symbolic incursion into territory that crosses gender boundaries' (Bullough and Bullough viii) and as such '(it) is a disruptive element that involves not just a category crisis of male and female, but the crisis of category itself' (325). Cross-dressing, therefore, places in crisis the time-honoured perception of what men and women should be and how they should act and, ultimately, challenges the male/female construct. Male cross-dressing, in particular, assumes a greater symbolic threat to patriarchal sex and gender differentiation, as it is the societally empowered male, the privileged male, who disempowers himself.

When a man casts off his clothes for those of the other, 'weaker' sex, he is symbolically showing that he is not a 'real man.' As such, he is voluntarily taking on an 'inferior' sex, gender, and social status by wearing female clothing. On wearing this other sex's clothing, the male cross-dresser would also seem to acquire unmanly qualities. As Jean E. Howard writes, quoting from Phillip Stubbes's *Anatomie of Abuses* (1583):

> For a man, wearing a woman's dress undermined the authority inherently belonging to the superior sex and placed him in a position of shame.
>
> At the simplest level, wearing effeminately ornate clothes would, in Stubbes' words, make men 'weake, tender, and infirme, not able to abide such sharp conflicts and blustering stormes' as their forefathers had endured (Stubbes 1583:E). At a more serious level, men actually wearing women's clothes, and not just ornate apparel, are so thoroughly 'out of place' that they become monstrous. (25)

In other words, it would seem that when a man wears female clothing, shamefully losing his privileged position in a patriarchal society, he takes on feminine characteristics that make him less of a man or not a man at all. Ultimately, he is converted into an 'inverted' anomaly of nature, a monster. The male cross-dresser becomes an 'aberration' according to the binary male/female order system as he is no longer strictly male or female. Judith Butler explains the ultimate effect of this in-between state of dress:

> Drag constitutes the mundane way in which genders are appropriated, theatricalized, worn, and done; it implies that all gendering is a kind of impersonation and approximation. If this is true, it seems, there is no original of primary gender that drag imitates, but *gender is a kind of imitation for which there is no original*; in fact, it is this kind of imitation that produces in the very notion of the original as an *effect* and consequence of the imitation itself. ('Imitation and Gender Insubordination' 21)

This in-between state of dress challenges the existence and validity of gender categories seen as sacrosacnt to society and its control, whether in the baroque era or contemporary society. Cross-dressing represents, therefore, a visually symbolic and bona fide threat to the regulating binaries of heterocentric society.

Howard highlights the importance that a strict and engendered dress code played in the control of society in seventeenth-century Europe:

> Dress, as a highly semiotic system, became a primary site where a struggle over the mutability of the social order was conducted ... The stability of the social order depends on maintaining absolute distinctions as much between male and female as between aristocrat and yeoman. (23)

Dress, therefore, was not only a question of class distinction but, more important for this study, of gender differentiation. Indeed, for Howard, gender relations were relations of power that ensured the division of labour in favour of the 'dominant gender' (25). For our purposes, gender and the vestimentary system that went with it were used to oppress women. Butler further strengthens Howard's argument, stating that '[t]he economy that claims to include the feminine as the subordinate term in a binary opposition of masculine/feminine excludes the feminine, produces the feminine as that which must be excluded for that economy to operate' (*Bodies that Matter* 36). Further, the need to uphold this sex and gender construct, apart from the important economic advantages for the 'on top' men, was based on the fear of disorder, of losing control:

The strict binary delineation of the sex/gender system of masculine and feminine provides an ordered classification schema against which the only alternative seems to be uncontainable elasticity and a chaotic and terrifying lack of boundaries within or between human bodies. (Epstein and Straud 14)

It would seem, however, that some slippage in dress codes was in fashion during the sixteenth and seventeenth centuries:

Cross dressing and impersonation, or playing with gender, was an increasingly important theme in the sixteenth and seventeenth century, emphasizing that gender differences were more flexible than they appeared. (Bullough and Bullough 74)

Significantly, therefore, it would seem that a slippage in the traditional means of controlling society, dress codes, and therefore sex and gender roles, was not unusual. The imperative need by the powers that be to control and enforce dress codes during this period thus becomes more apparent.

Baroque Spain in particular represented a period of history where societal roles in general were in great flux. One of the main moral issues of the day was the changing representation of what a man should be and, on the flip side, a woman's position in society. Many moralists considered that the Spanish empire was failing due to the lack of real men; gender and sexual roles for men were seen to be in crisis and hence so was Spain and its empire. This crisis represented a social and political change in Spain where the once combative chivalrous male had become a more leisurely and passive urban and courtly player. At the forefront was the fear of the so-called effeminization of the urban male so given to dressing up and engaging in frivolous activity and other behaviours not worthy of a man, namely homosexual relations. In many instances, the discussions concerning what could be called an era of a new masculinity or, in the minds of many, a weakened, effeminate one, became the theme of many moralists' writings and of Spanish baroque theatre. The cross-dressing male with his inherent power to shock, entertain, and 'engender' confusion became a vehicle for fostering further questioning and a means to expose a new and questionable masculinity.[2]

Of course, the theatrical male cross-dresser, while feared for this converting/inverting potential, has served from the beginning of theatre as an effective means to question the contradictions and injustices of the male/female dyad:

> From Plato's condemnation of playing the other (a fear that mimetic free-dom was formative, men might tend to become the women they imitate on stage) to the Puritanical anti-theatrical tracts of the English Renaissance, the human body has been a site for repression and possession. Theatrical cross-dressing has provided one way of playing with liminality and its multi-ple possibilities and extending that sense of the possible to the spectator/reader; a way of play, that while often reinforcing the social mores and status quo, carries with it the possibility for exposing that liminal moment, that threshold of questioning, that slippery sense of a mutable self. (Ferris 9)

Marjorie Garber further highlights that 'Renaissance antitheatricalists, in their debates about gender, cross-dresing, and the stage, articulated deep-seated anxieties about the possibility that identity was not fixed, that there was no underlying 'self' at all, and that therefore identities had to be zealously and jealously safeguarded' (32). In the gender-bending *entremeses* studied in this chapter, Juan Rana evokes the subver-sive questioning of sex and gender roles and meaningful mayhem that has always surrounded the cross-dressing male.

What must be remembered, however, in the case of Juan Rana, is the fact that the actor's cross-dressing is staged purely for public consump-tion. In collusion with the many playwrights who wrote for him, Juan Rana furthered his career by agreeing to be cross-dressed. The cross-dressing *entremeses* written specifically for the actor were used as a vehicle to parody social, political, sex, gender, marital, and biological roles already in crisis in baroque Spain and not as a display of Juan Rana's proclivity to wearing female clothing. Undeniably, however, the actor's well-known homosexuality, a sexuality often and mistakenly linked to cross-dressing, allowed for this theatrical male femaling in a nonthreat-ening manner. While today cross-dressing can be considered in its vari-ous subprocesses of ' "displaying," "disclosing," "passing," "reading," and "pretending" (Ekins 48–9), and in many cases as a stage in the process of sex-changing, this was not the case for Juan Rana. Juan Rana performed in female clothing not only as a means to an economic end but also as a way to expose the injustice of sex and gender roles. Lesley Ferris explains that '[c]ross-dressing in performance is riddled with dissension and ambiguity. Contemporary drag, for example, answers to a viable gay aesthetic while simultaneously promulgating misogynistic images of women ...; the staple image-making of male drag performers relies on grotesque caricature' (9). In the case of Juan Rana his performance is undoubtedly 'riddled with dissension and ambiguity' and in many ways presents a 'grotesque caricature' of women. But unlike contemporary drag, the intentions of the playwrights and Juan Rana are not to demean women with misogynistic representation. On the contrary, the analysis of the Juan Rana *entremeses* of this chapter, *La boda de Juan Rana, Juan Rana muger* (Cáncer y Velasco 1676), and *El parto de Juan Rana* (Lanini y Segredo c. 1668), show that sex and gender identity, like clothes, are 'put on' and that women in general are victims of patriarchical dress codes.

Before entering into the textual analysis of the cross-dressing Juan Rana, it is imperative to consider his ever-present counterpart, the masculine woman. Gail Bradbury insightfully points out that this particular male/female coupling was of great interest to the inquisitive scientist and dramatist of the Golden Age:

> Clearly, the scientists of the age were not at all reluctant to associate the masculine woman and the effeminate man with at least two abnormalities – sex-change and 'mixed sexuality' – which shock *our* society. It would therefore be unreasonable to suppose that seventeenth-century dramatists avoided, of necessity, the more sensational aspects of the strong woman/weak man topic, or that their audiences were less aware than we are of the blurred boundaries between 'inverted' and 'irregular' sexuality. (567)

Juan Rana and his gender-bending relationship with his domineering theatrical wife is an excellent example of the sexual abnormality that so fascinated the baroque scientist and dramatist alike. Susan C. Shapiro considers the question of sexual abnormality as it pertains to traditional sex, gender, and marital roles:

> Although *known* homosexuality always implied 'effeminacy' ... the reverse is simply not the case. 'Effeminacy' traditionally was associated with weakness, softness, delicacy, enervation, cowardice, delight in luxurious food and clothing – all those qualities that oppose the essential attributes of the warrior, the most 'manly' of men. But just as frequently, 'effeminacy' was used to connote some deviant form of *hetero*sexuality: subservience to a wife or mistress, lecherousness, or the compulsive pursuit of sexual experience to the neglect of more 'manly' activities ... or conversely, such personal

vanity and self-absorption as to preclude any but the feeblest interest in sexuality at all. (Shapiro 400–2 cited in MacFarlane 43)

Cameron MacFarlane adds further fuel to the theory of unmanliness by arguing that

the manliness/effeminacy distinction translates into power/weakness, activeness/passivity. Effeminacy, in other words, has less to do with what a man might adopt – frilly clothes, rarefied notions – than with what he abandons – power, mastery, control. This is why the plainly dressed man subservient to his wife and even the lecherous, compulsive 'sex maniac' can be described as effeminate: they have both relinquished that mastery over the self and others that characterizes manliness. The ideological underpinning here, obviously, is the conventional masculinist gender hierarchy that constructs men as active, powerful, and dominant, and women as passive, weak, and subordinate in all things including, and I stress this, sexual intercourse. (43)

Importantly, this weak man/strong woman paradigm in all its ramifications serves as an important theoretical base for the Juan Rana *entremeses* where the bumbling, weak protagonist is dictatorially outwitted by the smarts and the strong will of his wife. Undeniably, it underlines Juan Rana's 'irregular' sexuality, be it on or off the stage.

La boda de Juan Rana by Gerónimo de Cáncer y Velasco first appeared in *Flor de entremeses, bayles y loas: Escogidos de los mejores Ingenios de España*, published in Zaragoza in 1676.[3] Cáncer's depiction of the match-making preambles to marriage is by no means traditional, as is to be expected of this *entremesista*[4] and a Juan Rana–specific *entremés*. The title alone brings attention to itself in a subtle way. Instead of the traditional focus given to the woman on 'her' wedding day, here the title centres on the fact that this special day will be 'his day.' This inferred antitraditional gender slant of the title plays itself out in the *entremés* in a gender-bending fashion. Indeed, *La boda*, through the use of cross-dressing, inverts the highly semiotic system of dress and marriage in the baroque era. In *La boda*, Juan Rana plays the role of a mayor, as in many of his *entremeses*, but here he has not yet acquired his infamous wife sidekick. *La boda* represents, therefore, a rarity in the Juan Rana repertoire, in the sense that the Juan Rana mayor character is not depicted as a henpecked husband. What we find, however, is a Juan Rana who, while at first reluctant to enter into marriage, is finally persuaded to do so when his friend finds a partner for him much to his liking. In this way, we witness an unmarried Juan Rana voluntarily entering into an irregular marriage.

At the beginning of *La boda*, Juan Rana's fellow actor Simón Aguado brings up the subject of marriage or, more precisely, the fact that the protagonist is not yet married. From his negative reaction, this is quite obviously a prickly subject for Juan Rana. It would seem that Juan Rana has been putting off getting married. Simón points out that 'todo el lugar entero te ha notado' (148), that his constituents have noted his 'irregular' marital status. Juan Rana's subsequent comment, '[Es] mi boda processo' (149), shows him to believe his wedding day to be like a trial – an extraordinary event that everyone is anxiously waiting to witness. Simón points out that '[e]n fin es mucha mengua/ que en hombre tan honrado pongan lengua' (149) or, in other words, it is not good for the reputation of an honourable man like Juan Rana that he be the centre of gossip and attention. What we experience, therefore, in the opening lines of this *entremés* are the societal pressures placed on the unmarried Juan Rana to conform to the status quo. Considering the actor's well-known arrest for the *pecado nefando*, the spectator would surely understand this commentary on the need to keep up appearances. This is, of course, the result of a *qué dirán* (what will the neighbours say) society where appearances are of the utmost importance – one cannot appear to be different, to not conform to heterocentric values. In the end, Juan Rana will find his match thanks to the efforts of Simón, but his better half will be by no means traditional.

Simón has taken Juan Rana's undesirable bachelorhood situation into his own hands and arranged a marriage for him. On telling him of the impending marriage, Simón would seem to be trying to convince Juan Rana of his choice of bride by detailing some of her qualities. Juan Rana, however, is not easily swayed, as we can see by his antagonistic comments about the bride he has not seen yet. To Simón's verbal exaltation of the betrothed's 'hermosura' (beauty), Juan Rana sarcastically replies, 'Buena alhaja por Christo, para esposa' (150) (By God, what a prize of a wife). There is a sharp misogynist edge to his comment if we consider that *alhaja* (a word synonymous with *joya*, or jewel) is not only a generic object of value, but also an object of value used for personal adornment. The use of this word implies, therefore, that women are mere possessions and are at best purely decorative. Stronger still, however, is that *buena alhaja* is an ironic term used disdainfully to denote persons with a bad reputation for being cheats or liars or being otherwise mixed up in some sort of undesirable business. Juan Rana's first insult is indeed cutting and debasing to this woman and to women in general.

Subsequently, Juan Rana's friend comments on this woman's singing ability, to which the protagonist replies, 'Achaquitos padece de garganta?' (150) (Mustn't she have a terrible voice?). This reply is equally pejorative as Juan Rana is saying that her voice surely sounds as if she is suffering from some illness, affliction, or deformity of nature. In light of the misogynist angle of the text, it is perhaps no coincidence that metaphorically, *achaque* also refers to menstruation, once considered the curse of the 'weaker' sex. Simón now refers to a part of the body considered of great symbolic and erotic importance in the era, the foot. Simón exclaims, 'Que cristal y que pie soberano' (150) in reference to the transparency of this woman's skin and the finesse of her delicate feet. Juan Rana disdainfully replies, 'Mucho se passa ustè del pie à la mano' (150). Seemingly, Juan Rana underlines the fact that the alabaster-like colour of the beautifully formed foot, a sign of a noble upbringing, is not always reflected in the rest of the body. In addition, this utterance refers to his reluctance to ask for her hand in marriage. Once again his attitude is completely negative as he counters Simón's comments.

Yet another important and traditional aspect of alluring female beauty is described – the eyes. Simón states that the woman's eyes are between green and blue. Simón describes her eyes as a 'vision' of great beauty while Juan Rana would seem to find the idea of them a 'sight for sore eyes.' In reality, he does not comment on their present beauty but rather sees the grief they will cause him in the future. He states, 'A la vista esperanças de mis zelos' (150). In other words, the protagonist assumes that this woman will be unfaithful to him and that her eyes will only become an object of his future jealous scorn as the cuckolded husband. This is, of course, an underlying theme in many Juan Rana *entremeses*. Continuing in his description of the bride-to-be, Simón comments, 'En fin muger/ que tiene linda arenga' (150) (finally a woman/ with a silver tongue). Juan Rana in his rejection of this quality would seem to interpret *arenga* in the ironic sense as affected and impertinent chatter designed to persuade or deceive another in order to obtain what is desired. He believes, therefore, that this future wife will use her language skills to get what she wants, that she will be the conniving henpecking wife so very often seen in other Juan Rana *entremeses*.

In this bantering exchange between Simón and Juan Rana we have heard opposite opinions on the virtues of female beauty. All in all, this histrionic and hysterical battle of words serves to demythologize the démodé Renaissance code of female beauty. While Simón upholds this idealized code, acting as the straight man, as it were, Juan Rana is degrading, pessimistic, direct, and, indeed, earthy in his replies. His 'below-the-belt' humorous replies are quite fitting to the *entremés* but, at the same time, represent a negative topos prevalent in the Spanish baroque period. This reflection of baroque misogynism and the 'battle-of-the-sexes' topos are well entrenched in popular and literary culture and thus serve here as an effective device for raucous laughter. We have, therefore, a passé idealized code for female beauty mocked by a good measure of baroque cynicism and medieval earthiness. Another important element of the idealized Renaissance woman not yet considered, however, is the all-important question of chaste love.

On the subject of chastity, Simón is forced into telling Juan Rana the 'revealing' truth and the reasons behind his marital arrangement. When Simón explains, 'Principes soberanos/ desprecia por esposos à dos manos;/ solo à ti por Alcalde,/ sin interès te quiere' (150) (She rejects great princes/ aplenty;/ as mayor, disinterestedly/ she loves only you), he has perhaps gone too far in his accolades. Juan Rana cannot believe such a grandiose statement and suspiciously states, 'En algo su malicia/ se funda, pues me quiere por justicia' (150) (There must be something behind her wanting to marry me). Simón admits, 'Tuya es la conveniencia' (150) (This is advantageous for you). At this point Juan Rana asks a very direct and what would seem to be a normal question under the circumstances: 'Es muger de copete?/ incluye algunas faltas?' (151) (Is she stuck-up? [*also literally,* Does she wear her hair high in the front?]/ Does she have any faults?). We could get the impression that Juan Rana is innocently asking about his future wife's toilette, perhaps questioning if she 'puts on a false front' and asking if she has any faults. However, there is a more meaningful and less innocent interpretation of this line if we consider another metaphorical meaning of *copete*: anything which rises and curves like the *copete* hairstyle. This second meaning of *copete* 'coupled' with the use of a second meaning of *falta*, a month in which a woman does not menstruate because she is pregnant, refers to the 'rising' of the bride's stomach as her pregnancy advances. This condition would be, of course, quite obvious when Simón explains how many *faltas* there have been, 'solas siete' (151) (only seven). With the bride seven months pregnant, it becomes obvious why Simón was forced into telling the 'pregnant' truth. This pregnant analogue continues when Juan Rana states, 'De Noviembre à la fecha, con que espero,/ que parirà mi esposa por Enero' (151) (From this date in November, I expect,/ my wife will give birth in January). The last element of the Renaissance code for the ideal woman, chaste love, is most definitely mocked in this revealing exchange between Simón and Juan Rana. Here Simón's realistic comments contrast with his earlier ones that represented lofty Renaissance rhetoric.

At this point in the dialogue Simón would seem to reproach Juan Rana for his negative attitude towards his future wife, stating of her, 'No merece descalçarla' (151). *No merece descalçarla* is, on the one hand, a phrase used to describe a person who, according to the speaker, is not being given his or her due credit: in this case, the bride-to-be, who is not being given her due credit by Juan Rana. Therefore, Simón is stating, in the evangelical sense of the dictum, that Juan Rana should not take for granted what the good Lord has given him. Remembering, however, that this woman is already pregnant, 'no merece descalçarla' takes on a more literal and earthy meaning if we consider that *calzas* also refers to pants, or underclothing. This impregnated woman has quite clearly already lowered her knickers, making the virginal wedding night quite inapplicable. Juan Rana's next line puts the finishing touches on this play on words concerning pregnancy: 'Vozes que faltas no explican,/ son palabras muy preñadas' (151) (Words that cannot explain away *faltas,/* are very pregnant words). The unjustifiable *faltas* combined with the word *preñadas* make the out-of-wedlock pregnancy quite clear as, at seven months, it surely must have been to any observer.

The earlier play on words with *calças* and its derivatives takes on a significant semantic change in the subsequent short exchange between the two men. It would seem that the question of pregnancy is dropped for that of power. Simón explains that 'su esposa/ quiere calçarse las calças' (151). The mystery bride-to-be states up front that she wants to be the head and decision-maker of the household, that she wants 'to wear the pants' in the relationship. Traditionally, it is considered wrong and, indeed, *contra naturam*, that a woman should have a forceful disposition and strong character and indeed, be the head of the household, as Bradbury has indicated. This subordinate perception of women is obviously shown in the *mujer esquiva* (taming of the shrew) topos in baroque literature where the stubborn and headstrong woman is usually tricked if not beaten into submission. In the case of Juan Rana, however, no such controlling intervention takes place. Indeed, Juan Rana's reaction inverts this thematic convention and shows that this marriage of convenience is advantageous for both parties. It would seem that Juan Rana agrees in principle with his future wife's demand for an inverted marriage but he takes this metaphorical demand quite literally, as his reply indidates:

> Como ella me dexe à mi
> algun guardapies con plata,
> justillo correspondiente,
> y balona cariñana,
> la renuncio los calçones. (151)

> As long as she leaves me
> a hoopskirt embroidered in silver,
> the matching corset,
> and wimple,
> I'll surrender my pants to her.

In the end, Juan Rana would seem to be saying that if his future wife provides him with the necessary female clothing, he will indeed give up his powerful patriarchal pants. There is, therefore, much semantic play with the metaphorical and literal physical change of habits promised by Juan Rana. On one level, with his willingness to give up male clothing and to cross-dress, Juan Rana is metaphorically renouncing his right as a man to be the head of the family. Effectively, Juan Rana's cross-dressing amounts to theatrical cross-gendering – he has agreed to give up what is considered traditionally part of the role and duties of the male gender; he has agreed to a marital, sex, and gender change. Within the male/female construct of the period and indeed, of today, the idea of a male dressing as a female and, as such, relinquishing traditional phallocentric power would seem so unthinkable as to be monstrously hysterical. For this reason, the cross-dressed male continues to be an effective vehicle for laughter.

What would seem to be an unbelievable and hilarious cross-dressing fetish on the part of Juan Rana holds yet another layer of significance. The *guardapies* and *calçones* can hide the pregnancy of a woman[5] and the gender of a male cross-dresser. In the case of the *balona cariñana*, both gender and identity of the wearer can be hidden. It is as if Cáncer y Velasco, in his choice of clothes for Juan Rana's cross-dressing, has chosen those that are able to hide the body and its interior secrets, to keep them away from the eyes of the ever-judgmental societal gaze. At this point of the *entremés*, however, we are but tantalized by the prospect of Juan Rana's histrionic and hysterical cross-dressing. Before this climactic moment takes place, we must first meet his mystery bride-to-be.

We have heard a great deal about Juan Rana's future wife, but only in the abstract and codified terms of Renaissance female beauty and its demythologized opposite. We have yet to see her for ourselves. Coincidentally, after Juan Rana's verbal acceptance of her cross-dressing demands, the infamous woman herself, Inès, appears in the company of musicians and three gallants. On her entrance, the musicians sing her marriage demands:

> Quien quisiere ser marido
> de Inès, a fuer de las tablas,
> ha de permitir que sea
> muger de capa, y espada. (152)

> Whoever would attempt to be
> the husband of Inés, offstage
> must allow her to be
> a female swashbuckler.

There is, of course, a play on words with 'de capa, y espada' (of cape and sword). In theatrical terminology, this expression refers to a genre of plays, but interpreted literally, Inès is demanding to dress as a man, complete with the cliché symbol of phallic power, the sword. Once again, therefore, we learn that Inès wants to dress as the man and hence, be the man in the proposed relationship. The three gallants would all seem to be aghast at her nontraditional demand:

GALAN 1:   Proposicion muy terrible.
GALAN 2:   La condicion es terrible.
GALAN 3:   Yo me apartè de la empessa. (152)

GALLANT 1: Terrible proposal.
GALLANT 2: The condition is terrible.
GALLANT 3: I'm no longer in the game.

In this way, these potential suitors, in their astonishment at such a demeaning demand, represent the usual negative male reaction to Inès's proviso. The last *galán* would seem to speak for the three of them when he gives up on his quest to marry Inès. The musicians now sing about what Inès expects of her future husband:

> Busca Inès un marido
> como de almario
> pues quiere, sin que assombre, hombre
> para el estrado. (152)

> Inès seeks
> a trophy husband
> for she desires – let it amaze no one –
> a man to show off.

It would seem Inès wants a showpiece or decorative husband, and wants to be married only in the figurative sense, if we consider the meaning of *almario* and *estrado*. An *almario* is a fancy cabinet to show off one's prized possessions. *Estrado*, on the other hand, is a decorative object used by women in their boudoir. Inès's wish for a husband to decorate her parlour or boudoir parallels Juan Rana's earlier negative use of the word *alhaja* to describe women as decorative possessions. Inès is, therefore, inverting the misogynist code by considering men as mere objects. Simón would seem to sell this 'objective' quality in Juan Rana when he states, '[D]e cera no puede ser/ hombre de tan linda pasta/ como el que os traygo, señora' (152–3) (A man of wax could not be/ of more beautiful stuff/ than the one I bring you, lady). While this statement certainly objectifies Juan Rana as a beautiful waxen commodity, *pasta* also has a second meaning: metaphorically, it refers to a weak person. This second meaning befits the bumbling mayor persona that Juan Rana created and made so very famous.

As opposed to the *tres galanes* who quickly gave up the chance to wed Inès on hearing her conditions for marriage, Juan Rana is delighted with this nontraditional arrangement:

> JUAN RANA: En viendola basta
>   Yo soy, esposa, un marido,
>   que os viene à servir de dama
>   y tomad aquesta mano,
>   por toda aquesta semana.

INÈS: En darme la mano ya
                 reconozco la ventaja.
                 Sebeis que à ser mi marido
                 venis con las circunstancias
                 de que yo el mando, y el palo
                 he de tener en mi casa?
JUAN RANA: Y darame quanto pida?
INÈS: Aquello serà sin falta.
JUAN RANA: Pues llamenme desde luego
                 todos doña Juana Rana. (153)

JUAN RANA: Seeing her is enough.
                 I am, wife, a husband
                 who comes to serve you as a lady,
                 and take this hand,
                 for all this week.
INÈS: In giving your hand
                 I now see that I have the upper hand.
                 Do you know that to be my husband
                 you agree to the condition
                 that I will have control, and the stick
                 in my house?
JUAN RANA: And will you give me all I ask?
INÈS: This I swear.
JUAN RANA: Then from now on let everyone call me
                 Mrs Juana Rana.

This total acceptance of the marriage demands of Inès and, hence, the agreement to be the woman in the marriage, corresponds with Juan Rana's prior agreement to lose the *calzones*; to metaphorically and literally give up the pants/power of the family and replace them with women's (under)garments. Here he agrees that Inès will lead the family and hold the *palo*, an obvious phallic symbol of power. All this Juan Rana gladly gives up, taking on the subservient role of the wife who is provided for. Juan Rana, the symbolically self-castrated male, renames himself Doña Juana Rana.

La boda finally arrives at its climactic moment – the vestimentary transformation of Juan Rana into Doña Juana Rana and Inès into Don Inès. To draw attention to this event Simón exclaims, 'Plaça, plaça'

(Make way). The use of a command normally reserved for the passing of royalty and other important occasions, is in itself quite ironic. At the same time, however, the imperative *plaça* is the beginning of an important play on words that continues throughout this passage.

We can only imagine the raucous reaction of the audience to the spectacular dressing of Juan Rana by others as indicated in the stage directions: '*Visten de dama à Cosme, y Manuela queda de villano*' (153) (Cosme is dressed like a woman, and Manuela as a man). On the other hand, however, the actor's comments on his festive and public transformation into a woman are doubly meaningful and significant:

> Prende el justillo de suerte
> que descubra la garganta.
> Yo soy dama xavali,
> pues de telas me hazen plaça. (153)

> Tighten the corset so that
> it shows off my neck.
> I am a female boar,
> trapped in my clothes.

Juan Rana would seem to be indicating that he wants the *justillo* tightened in such a way that he have a more elongated bodily posture. In the first two lines of this passage, Juan Rana explains how this garment, a type of corset, is usually worn. At the same time he is mocking the fact that women are physically forced into a constraining and discomforting 'form' of beauty. This also relates to Inès's earlier wish for an *homre a justado* (cinched man tailored to her tastes). The female body, therefore, is not only beautifully constrained but is also made into a protected area fortified from the 'enemy' – like a *plaça* or fortified public square. This visual image of uncomfortable beauty takes on a more metaphorical meaning if we analyse the remaining lines of this passage for their double meanings.

Looking at the last line, *tela* is, of course, any type of cloth, but, significantly, it also means a cordoned-off area or corral used to enclose game in order to kill it in safety. Juan Rana through the utterance of double meanings is stating that he, like a 'dama xavali' or female boar, is entrapped by clothing. In addition, Juan Rana's vestimentary entrapment is very much a public spectacle. Hence, we see the meaningful link between the words *plaça* and *tela* that adroitly show the correlation between female clothing and entrapment. This passage is a comment on female clothing as a codifying and controlling agent. Here it can be interpreted to show specifically the situation of women who are physically and metaphorically trapped in their restricting 'prison' clothes.

Juan Rana's cross-dressing puts into question traditional male/female roles inside and outside marriage by revealing gender roles as something 'put on' like clothes. In other words, Juan Rana's cross-dressing shows sex, gender, and marital roles and restrictions to be constructs. In this way, *La boda*, with its inversion of the male/female dress code and, as such, of gender roles, represents a parodic threat to the traditional patriarchal value system, to the clearly delineated male/female dyad. This vestimentary affront to phallocentricism and gender dictums shows *La boda* to be very contemporary in its locus, giving a different spin to the adage 'clothes make the man.'

In Cáncer y Velasco's *Juan Rana muger*, published in the same collection as his *La boda de Juan Rana*, the adage 'clothes make the man' is equally put to the test. As in *La boda*, a cross-dressed/gendered marriage is arranged, but under very different circumstances. In *Juan Rana muger*, as opposed to *La boda de Juan Rana*, the protagonist is already married. His wife, Casilda, vindictively dresses her husband as a woman while he is sleeping. On his awaking and with the aid of her cohorts, Juan Rana is eventually tricked into believing he is a young woman. This pattern fits the many *entremeses* in which Juan Rana's wife plays a joke on her husband to avenge his slothful demureness and chauvinist attitude and actions towards her. As such, this *entremés*, like many other Juan Rana *entremeses*, uses metatheatre or, more precisely, multiple levels of reality as its main theatrical tool. In *Juan Rana muger*, it is the wife and her coconspirators who within the play become the manipulators of Juan Rana's reality. On a certain level, this new reality created by the actors would seem to give them artistic freedom within the bounds of the *entremés*. This illusion of freedom gives the spectator the impression that they are the creators of the play within the play, that their creation is separate from the main play, that they are the actors and the authors of this metatheatre presentation. As in *La boda*, cross-dressing allows gender, sexual identity, and roles to be questioned. Juan Rana's cross-dressing in this instance, however, is involuntary. This imposed identity and sex and gender change and, indeed, this crisis serves as a means to a very different end. The message of *Juan Rana muger*, while similar to that of *La boda*, is much greater in scale, cutting to the core of the problems of patriarchal power.

From the very beginning of the *entremés*, Casilda appears on stage dressed as a man and when asked why she is dressed this way answers:

> Aquesto ha sido
> hurtar la bendicion à mi marido;
> y para que lo entiendas,
> esto es querer tener Carnestolendas,
> porque mirando yo, que no me dexa
> salir de casa por hazerme vieja
> y que es tan grande bestia el majadero
> que yo le hago creer quanto yo quiero,
> me he puesto su vestido,
> y à èl el mio, porque esta dormido
> con tan pesado sueño. (154–5)

> I am dressed like this to
> get back at my husband;
> and so that you understand,
> this is to turn the tables on him,
> because I see that he doesn't let me
> leave the house, to control me,
> and that he's so stupid, the old fool,
> that I can make him believe anything I want,
> so I've put on his clothes,
> and put mine on him, while he's
> sleeping like a log.

It would seem by her explanation that Casilda is rebelling against the cruel tyranny of her bumbling and foolish husband. More specifically, in preplay action, Juan Rana has absurdly prohibited his wife from leaving the house. As such, he has made her a prisoner in her own home. As part of her plan to teach Juan Rana a lesson in equality and justice, she has switched clothes with him while he was napping. In her jubilant retaliation against his rule, Casilda feels as if she is celebrating *Carnestolendas*, otherwise known as carnival, the party-filled days before Lent where roles can be reversed. Her festive explanation qualifies her joyous feeling of freedom and revenge in religious terms and indicates the carnivalesque, topsy-turvy tone of this *entremés*. But unlike during carnival, where switching roles is voluntary, it is the cross-dressed wife who forcefully switches clothes with her husband. It is the wife in her rebellion against patriarchal dress and rule who consciously controls the situation. The fact that her cohorts, the barber and the blacksmith, readily go along with her mutinous plot gives weight to her side of the story. In their agreement to be active accessories to this cross-dressing fraud they are agreeing that the tyranny imposed by her husband is also wrong in their eyes. The full support of two archetypal male representatives of society is a symbolic endorsement of Casilda's actions against her husband. Indeed, their participation in thwarting Juan Rana's marital tyranny would seem to show that they too were victims, this time of his mayoral tyranny.[6] Significantly, Casilda emphasizes that with their assistance in persuading Juan Rana that he is a woman and she a man, they will all live in peace (155). They will all have reason to celebrate his fall from power and her rise to it.

During the plotting against his person and station in life, Juan Rana blissfully sleeps. From this dormant and ignorant state, he will soon awake, however, to a new and transformed reality just like theatre itself. This involuntary transformation of his sex and gender and, hence, societal status will cause a rude awakening both literally and, as the *entremés* progresses, metaphorically. Casilda's autocratic awakening call is just the beginning of Juan Rana's forced lifestyle change:

Juana, muchacha, Juana, no respondes?
duermes aun? y tal bellaqueria;
despierta moza, que es ya medio dia. (155)

Juana, my girl, Juana, why don't you answer?
Are you still sleeping? what a bad girl;
wake up, girl, it's already noon.

Quite obviously, Casilda now takes on a commanding voice accusing the sleeping Juana of being lazy and misbehaving; in fact, throughout the *entremés*, Juan Rana is degradingly chastised through the use of misogynist and demeaning adjectives. The transfer of authority heard in Casilda's authoritative use of language is also heard in the use of the feminine of Juan, Juana. The sex/gender/power switch is also symbolically seen by the significant change of a particular piece of clothing as Juan Rana remarks: 'Mas que veo. Jesus, que ilusiones!/ Casilda, os habais puesto mis calçones?' (156) (Oh my God, am I seeing things?/ Casilda, have you put on my pants?). While in *La boda de Juan Rana* this vestimentary and symbolic transfer of the 'power pants' was the spectacular motor of the *entremés*, here it is only mentioned in passing by Juan Rana. However, the combination of oral and vestimentary signs makes it clear that Casilda has taken and put on the masculine role and, as such, she is well on her way to engendering a change in her husband.

Incredibly, Casilda does not wish Juan Rana to believe that they have merely switched marital roles, but rather, that he is her younger sister, Juana, and that she is his older brother, Benito. What ensues is a series of inversions that show that Juan Rana is no match for his wife. Continuing in the position of brotherly power, Casilda subserviently scolds Juan Rana for not being awake sooner and not having started dinner or, in other words, for not doing what is considered woman's work. Earlier in the *entremés* Calsida told her coconspirators that Juan Rana had dreamed that he was a woman on three consecutive nights. This fantasy most certainly sets the stage for Juan Rana's transformation, but Casilda in her plan to cross-gender her husband now inverts his dream reality:

> JUAN RANA: Yo soy Juana?
> CASILDA: Pues no lo vès, te olvidas de tu nombre?
>   ò has soñado esta noche, que eres hombre?
>   no te vès con corpiños, y manteo? (156)

> JUAN RANA: I am Juana?
> CASILDA: Isn't it obvious, have you forgotten your name?
>   or did you dream last night that you were a man?
>   can't you see you're wearing a corset and slip?

Considering Casilda's inversion of her husband's reality, it is logical that she should try to convince Juan Rana that as a young girl he has dreamed about being a man. Incredibly, therefore, Casilda causes her husband to experience two gender inversions, one in real life and one in his world of dreams. Most certainly, Casilda gives a new inverted twist to the idea of gender-bending.

Casilda's gender-bending efforts make the confused Juan Rana question his new reality and the relationship he has with his wife:

> Pues si soy Rana, claro es que soy hembra,
> mas si somos hermanos deste lado,
> con que dispensacion nos han casado? (157)

> If my last name is Rana, it's clear that I am female,
> but if on the other hand we're siblings,
> how is it that we got married?

While understanding that his last name, *rana* (literally, frog), is a feminine noun, thus projecting femininity onto him, Juan Rana does not comprehend how it came about that he is both sibling and spouse to Casilda. This passage clearly shows Juan Rana's confused state and the fact that his gender inversion by his wife is still in progress. At this point, Casilda announces that he is not only a female, but a 'doncella' or, in other words, a young maiden. This fact will act as the motor of the rest of the *entremés* and serve as the prime means to expose the plight of women within patriarchal society.

The barber now arrives to comment on the unkempt state of the house and to demand from Juana Rana the shirts that he had supposedly ordered from her. Juan Rana is once again astonished by the fact that he should be employed as a seamstress, a job typically reserved for a woman. He, of course, has not completed the imaginary shirt order. Next, Casilda's other cohort, the blacksmith, arrives to comment on another traditional female occupation – wool spinning. In this case, he is asking for his spun and threaded wool but, once again, Juana Rana has obviously not completed the made-up order. Apart from the fact that young women were typically employed in these two types of cottage industries, there is another conceptual play on words being 'spun' here. Inasmuch as both the seamstress and the wool-spinner work with *hilo* (thread), it would seem that Juan Rana is being made to *seguir el hilo* – he is being strung along. On another level of interpretation, as mayor he would have been well seasoned in the art of *hilar*, or spinning a yarn. This passage does, indeed, put a new 'spin' on the art of oratory. This conceptual play on words could also represent the material used by Casilda to weave the cross-dressed/gendered trap for her husband. Of course, we are considering two aspects of making clothes, sewing and spinning. They are integral parts of the vestimentary industry that manufactures gender identities and roles.

A new character, the old man, the so-called father of Juana and Benito, suddenly announces himself from offstage. The reason for his visit is quite clear from the very moment he speaks: 'Hija, ya que es tiempo de tomar estado' (159), or, it is now time for 'Juana' to be married off. Butler in her commentary on Claude Lévi-Strauss's theory of kinship (see Lévi-Strauss, 'The Principles of Kinship') explains the meaning of this new demand on the transformed Juan Rana:

The bride, the gift, the object of exchange constitutes 'a sign and a value' that opens a channel of exchange that not only serves the *functional* purpose of facilitating trade but performs the *symbolic* or *ritualistic* purpose of consolidating the internal bonds, the collective identity, of each clan differentiated through the act. In other words, the bride functions as a relational term between groups of men; she does not *have* an identity, and neither does she exchange one identity for another. She *reflects* masculine identity precisely through being the site of its absence. Clan members, invariably male, invoke the prerogative of identity through marriage, a repeated act of symbolic differentiation. (*Gender Trouble* 38–9)

The traditional commodification of young maidens by patriarchal society gives a new twist to the *entremés*'s message. Juan Rana, faced with a paternal authority figure who holds the power to command his future, forgets his earlier gender questionings: 'Yo estoy turbada, que soy muy niña yo para casada' (159) (I'm very confused, I'm too young to be married). Juan Rana himself now uses the feminine past participle to describe his troubled state and to explain that he, as a mere child, is too young to be married off; he is employing a typical ruse used to try to stop the paternally imposed marriage process. He states that he wants to become a nun. The father rejects this wish, saying that it is too late, now that suitors have already been lined up. When told that the future husband will sleep with him, Juan Rana tries desperately to explain that he has not been taken to the baths that day and that consequently, he does not have 'buenos bajos' (160). On one level Juan Rana is referring to not having been bathed that day and as such his *bajos* or undergarments are not as clean as they should be. On the level of Juan Rana playing a cross-dressed character, however, the spectator could interpret this line to mean that he literally does not have the right 'lower parts' beneath his female underclothes. Behind the hilarity of this scene, Juan Rana would seem to be mimicking the normal reactions of a terrified young virgin who has just been told that she must marry. In a comical way, therefore, Juan Rana is representing the fearful reality of many young girls, thrust into marriage by their fathers.

Regardless of the excuses and protests by Juan Rana, the old man is determined to marry off his daughter that very evening. This paternal haste would seem to underline the idea that woman are property without a say in their own future. As such, all decisions concerning the future must be made for them by others. This proximate marriage predicament causes Juan Rana to speak of another very real fear for women:

JUAN RANA: Pregunto, padre, y me he de hazer preñada?
VEGETE: Pues para que te casas, bobarrona?

JUAN RANA: Y he de parir?
VEGETE: Pues esso no te infiere?
JUAN RANA: El diablo lleve lo que yo pariere. (160)

JUAN RANA: I ask, father, do I have to become pregnant?
OLD MAN: Why else would you get married, silly girl?
JUAN RANA: And do I have to give birth?
OLD MAN: Isn't that obvious?
JUAN RANA: The devil take what I spawn.

On one level, Juan Rana is expressing the fear of a virginal girl who with little or no carnal knowledge is about to enter into sexual relations. With this passage, however, we have struck on a very important biological difference between men and women – women bear the burden of birth. This difference is what can be considered the great divide between men and women. Therefore, young women must be married off to order to reproduce but at the same time they must quickly be married off to avoid out-of-wedlock pregnancies and, hence, the loss of family honour. Juan Rana's fear as a young maiden is not for her honour, but rather, for the terrible physical pain of giving birth. This trepidation will take on a more dire angle later in the *entremés*. As before, the old man is oblivious to the worries and, indeed, the well-being of his daughter. He blindly continues with his marriage plans for her. The passage ends on a comical note aimed, once again, at the knowing spectator – Juan Rana hopes that the devil takes away the fruit of his loins.

At this moment in *Juan Rana muger*, the old man produces two pro-spective husbands from which Juana Rana must choose. The first is quickly rejected by the young bride to be:

VEGETE: Este es un caçador.
JUAN RANA: Pues no le quiero,
                        Porque me matará. (160)

OLD MAN: This one's a hunter.
JUAN RANA: Well I don't want him,
                        Because he'll kill me.

Juan Rana would seem to be afraid of an undesirable and life-threaten-ing marriage with a hunter. This hints, of course, at the reality of domestic violence against women who in those times would have no recourse from this marital predicament. The second candidate is also cast aside but on more comical grounds. When told that the second suitor is a *monacillo* or choir boy, Juan Rana states:

> JUAN RANA: La mitad me agrada.
> (MONACILLO): Pues porque la mitad?
> JUAN RANA: La mona quiero,
>   y el cillo que se quede en el tintero. (160)

> JUAN RANA: I half like him.
> (MONACILLO): Why only half?
> JUAN RANA: The top half's okay,
>   but I've no use for the bottom half.

The word *monacillo* here is divided into two parts, *mona* and *cillo*, in order to allow a play on words. Juan Rana likes the *mona* part, which familiarly refers to being drunk, but not the *cillo*, which he dismisses, using a reference to inkwells and quills, an obvious reference to coupling.

Notwithstanding the rejection of the two suitors, the old man forces Juan Rana to choose a husband. Juan Rana's final choice of the barber allows for different levels of double meanings:

> Pues si alguno ha de ser, venga el Barbero,
> que es hombre que con barbas no se ataja,
> y yo he menester mucha navaja. (160–1)

> If I have to choose somebody, let it be the barber,
> who's a man who doesn't get put off by beards,
> because I'll surely need a razor.

On one level of interpretation, *atajar* can mean to shave. In this sense, therefore, Juan Rana refers to the fact that the barber is accustomed to shaving off beards and he, the 'bride-to-be,' will be in great need of a barber's razor. This gives a new meaning to the concept of the 'bearded lady.' On a second level, however, *atajarse* means to verbally impose oneself on others. Also, *navaja* metaphorically refers to wagging tongues that cut like a knife. And finally, *barbas* is used to refer to an older and wiser man such as the old man.[7] In other words, on a comical second rendering, Juan Rana has chosen the barber as future partner for his ability to verbally defend 'him' against his father and other authority figures.

The courtship progresses to the point where the barber proposes. What ensues is clever hand and word play between him and Juan Rana:

BARBERO: Pues aquesta es mi mano, prenda mia.
JUAN RANA: No puedo yo dezir esso de la mia.
BARBERO: Porque no has de dezillo, bella ingrata?
JUAN RANA: Porque no sè si es mano, ò si es patata.
BARBERO: Mano es, y mano que yo estimo, y quiero.
JUAN RANA: Pues vesle ay una mano de mortero. (161)

BARBER: Here is my hand, my precious.
JUAN RANA: I can't say that of mine.
BARBER: Why can't you say it, you ungrateful girl?
JUAN RANA: Because I don't know if it is a hand or a potato.
BARBER: It's a hand, and a hand that I greatly esteem and love.
JUAN RANA: Well, here's my fat paw.

Of course, the hand offered by the barber is figuratively the promise of marriage. But Juan Rana hesitates to reciprocate, implying that his hand in marriage is not his own to bestow. This interpretation follows the idea of paternal ownership and control of the daughter that we have seen up to now. The barber, however, in calling Juan Rana 'bella ingrata,' would seem to interpret Juan Rana's response to mean that he does not wish the barber's hand in marriage. Comically, however, Juan Rana finally clears up the misunderstanding of the previous lines. From the beginning he was referring to the unattractiveness of his hand that resembles, in his mind, a potato. This is perhaps a reference to the round, rude, and unfeminine shape of his hand. With this misunderstanding cleared up, *El barbero* assures Juan Rana that his hand symbolically and otherwise is, indeed, worthy of his praise and love. In the next line spoken by Juan Rana, there is yet another play on words, typical of Juan Rana's earthy and festive responses. *Mortero* was a term used humorously to allude to short, chubby people; in other words, when Juan Rana uses *de mortero* he is alluding to his own short and stubby body. This bodily self-description corresponds to the actor's true physiognomy as can be seen in his caricatural portrait. A hand resembling the rounded potato, as Juan Rana described his own hand, would surely correspond to his body type.

In the end, Juan Rana concedes that he is a woman and agrees, under paternal pressure, to marry. In the same breath, however, the fear of giving birth, expressed earlier in terms of physical pain, now takes on a more serious tone:

CASILDA: Calla necia;
            Dudas que eres muger?
JUAN RANA: Ya sè que es cierto,
            mas esto del parir me tiene muerto.
VEGETE: Ea, llevalda, vuestro amor la vença.
JUAN RANA: No quiero padre, que tendrè verguença. (161)

CASILDA: Be quiet, fool;
            You doubt you are a woman?
JUAN RANA: Now I know it's true,
            but this idea of giving birth scares me to death.
OLD MAN: She's yours, your love will win her over.
JUAN RANA: I don't want to, father, I'm ashamed.

Indeed, Juan Rana is 'afraid to death' at the prospect of giving birth. This has been, of course, a reality as many women suffered and died while giving birth, as Nicky Hart has shown.[8] The father, once again oblivious to the feminine voice, answers that love will aid in overcoming this fear. After the old man's final show of paternal tyranny and disregard for his 'daughter's' wishes and fears, the barber announces the entry of all the neighbouring women to congratulate her on the upcoming wedding. What ensues is a musical and moralistic conclusion to this exemplary *entremés*.

First a woman sings of Juan Rana's turn of fate:

Mil vezes enhorabuena
estè de novio Juan Rana,
que ya de Alcalde perpetuo
aquesta boda le saca. (161)

A thousand congratulations,
to Juan Rana the intended,
who because of this marriage
is no longer the perpetual mayor.

Her festive voice is not celebrating the wedding of Juan Rana but rather what results from it – she is celebrating his demise from power. In her anonymity, she sings for all disempowered women but at the same time her voice is that of the people. With Juan Rana inverted and transformed into a young bride-to-be, he has lost his mayor-for-life position, a posi-

tion that he had abused. The individualized voice of Juan Rana's wife
also has some final words of wisdom:

> CASILDA: El marido que encierra,
> La muger en la casa,
> sino vè lo que passa,
> mete dentro de guerra;
> y ella, que no lo yerra,
> por la mano le gana.
> Que se case Juan Rana. (162)

> CASILDA: The husband who locks
> his wife up at home,
> if he isn't careful,
> he'll have a war on his hands;
> and she, making no mistake,
> by her skill will defeat him.
> Let Juan Rana be married.

In essence, Casilda is warning the male members of the public that, if
they lock up their wives or mistreat them in any way they will pay for their
folly. She continues to caution that women will not err in righting that
which is unjust. While in the body of the text we experienced a histrionic
and humourous example of mistreatment, we now have the forewarning
and serious voice of female experience. She is the voice that imparts the
moral of the story. Here we have the voice of a mature woman as opposed
to the inverted example of a tyrannized and innocent maiden. Here *mano*
suggests Casilda's dexterity in changing her husband into a *doncella*. It
would seem, however, that the overall meaning of this passage alludes to
the strength of women in general to skilfully outwit their bullish husbands.

Finally, Juan Rana, who was indeed outwitted by his wife, reiterates his
wife's message:

> Casese noramala.
> La muger que se quiere
> escapar del marido,
> quando la ha sacudido
> à si mismo se hiere,
> porque quando bolviere
> le çurre la badana. (162)

Marry at your own peril.
When he mistreats a wife
who will try to escape him,
a husband only
hurts himself,
for when she comes back
she'll make him pay.

In this way, Juan Rana states that the man who mistreats his wife is actually hurting himself, as he will eventually pay both verbally and physically for his wrongdoings. The Juan Rana of the musical finale has been returned back to his gendered self. He has, however, learned from first-hand experience the fears and plight of many young women.

As a whole, therefore, the *entremés* can be seen to be divided into two main sections, the main body of the text and the summarizing song. While both serve to teach men a lesson about their (mis)treatment of women, the manner of relating this message is quite different. In the main text, the spectator learns by seeing an exaggerated and inverted example of the abuse of power. In the sung finale, on the other hand, the spectator directly hears this same message by the actors now reverted to their 'true' gender although still within the confines of characterization. If in the main body of the *entremés*, the feminine voice of the cross-dressed/gendered Juan Rana is exaggeratedly and parodically ignored, in the concluding musical moments it is heard loudly and clearly. It is the female characters who dominate this melodious finale. Through song they emphasize that the man of the house cannot arbitrarily imprison and disempower his better half without the risk of going to battle against the person he has despotically made his enemy.

Through the inverted revolt staged by his wife, Juan Rana has lost his power in the microcosm of marriage and the macrocosm of his municipality. His misuse of marital and municipal power has cost him both positions of patriarchal authority. Through his tyranny, paralleled by the actions of the old man, he has forced upon himself a revolt by his wife and constituents. He has received a lesson in the importance of equality and justice for all that, while centred in his marriage, goes beyond this familiar unit. As such he becomes a *pharmakos* and a message for the spectator. Ultimately, *Juan Rana muger* is a lesson directed not only to husbands but to all those who hold a position of power. This exposé of the underlying ills of a patriarchal society is clearly a message of empowerment to women but, at the same time, to all underlings.

Pedro Francisco Lanini y Segredo's *El parto de Juan Rana* also puts into question gender and identity roles within a patriarchal context, but this *entremés* goes one step further into the realm of gender-bending fantasy.[9] If, in *Juan Rana muger*, Juan Rana is tricked into believing that he is a maiden terrified by the prospect of marriage, sexual relations, pregnancy, and giving birth, here he is an experienced and entrapped spouse who histrionically endures labour pains in the act of giving birth on stage. Indeed, with this *entremés* we enter into questions of biological differences between men and women and the legal ramifications of crossing the biological and gender line.

Significantly, Juan Rana does not appear until close to the end of the *entremés*. This delay creates a measure of temporal, thematic, and theatrical expectancy on the part of the audience. Like anxious parents-to-be, therefore, the audience must wait for the spectacular arrival of Juan Rana and the climactic childbirth. On another level, however, this pregnant absence shows the drawing power of the Juan Rana name and the fact that his persona has a life of its own. Juan Rana's significant absence allows for a lively discussion among his mayoral peers concerning his *façon d'être* and present pregnant condition. The meeting of municipal leaders to decide the fate of Juan Rana is not unlike a meeting of the Inquisition and the grilling he surely received when arrested for the *pecado nefando*.

El parto begins with a scribe announcing to Cosme Berrueco, the mayor of Meso, that he has been chosen to be head judge in the in absentia trial of Juan Rana. The name of this presiding mayor is significant. On one level, the adjective *berrueco* refers to a rude and rough rocky area. This could be a topographical reference that symbolizes his manner and origin. This adjective also refers to an imperfect pearl with an irregular surface and considered of little value. This too could refer to his rough and poor background. This adjective could also refer to the skin of this particular mayor who had suffered the skin-deforming disease, smallpox, common in this era. Notwithstanding, he, as the head judge, symbolizes the poor background and limited intelligence of the other five mayors who will soon arrive on the scene.

ESCRIBANO: A vos Cosme Berrueco
            (insigne Alcalde del lugar de Meso),

a vos os han nombrado
los concejos, por juez tan afamado,
para que presidais en esta Audencia,
en que a tomar se viene residencia
al Alcalde Juan Rana,
que preso tienen por la más liviana
fea culpa que Alcalde ha cometido:
despúes que Alcaldes en consejo ha habido:
su cargo es enormísimo. (426)

SCRIBE: Cosme Berrueco,
(illustrious mayor of Meso),
you have been named
by the council, for being such a noted judge,
to preside over this audience,
to pass judgment on
Mayor Juan Rana,
who is detained for the most wanton
and heinous crime that any mayor has committed
since mayors have been in office:
your responsibility is enormous.

From this solemn and official proclamation by the scribe, we learn that
the powers-that-be have imprisoned Juan Rana because they consider
him to have committed the most vile of all crimes.[10] While it is not
mentioned outwardly at this point, from the title of the *entremés* it can be
assumed that the scribe is referring to Juan Rana's pregnancy. Indeed, as
Juan Rana's condition quite obviously goes against the laws of nature,
the scribe's attitude would seem quite in tune with the era's ideas of the
control of sexual mores. The council will try, therefore, to right this
contra naturam crime by means of man-made laws. Berrueco questions,
however, whether Juan Rana's *contra naturam* pregnancy, an absurd
impossibility, is less horrid than another crime against nature that is an
integral part of Juan Rana's persona/person:

Escribano,
no seais vos inormismo: á la mano
os id: es mas la culpa encreminada
enormisma, fea y ponderada

el que Juan Rana (porque á nadie se asombre)
para hembra es mejor que para hombre? (427)

Scribe,
do not exaggerate: stop
right there: isn't the greater,
more heinous and more unthinkable crime
that Juan Rana (let no one be taken by surprise)
is better suited to being a woman than a man?

With the use of *inormísmo*, Berrueco is using a legal term that refers to price-gouging where the mark-up is more than 50 per cent of the merchandise's value; namely, he is telling the scribe not to exaggerate when speaking of this particular crime. There is, of course, a humorous element to this use, as this term is also similar to the the term *enormísimo*, the superlative of *enorme*, a reference to Juan Rana's full-term and showing pregnancy. In his wisdom as head judge, Berrueco asks which crime is greater, Juan Rana's pregnancy as a man or the well-known and, hence, unsurprising fact that he is better suited to being a woman. While in the context of the *entremés*, this womanliness refers to the fact that Juan Rana performs woman's work, it is quite probably a reference to his on- and offstage gayness. The hilarity of this theatrical posturing – that the biological impossibility of male pregnancy be weighed against a man playing the woman's role in marriage and by extension, of being un-manly and/or gay – reflects the absurdity of strict gender roles. It also represents a gay and subversive attack against the church and state.

The pretrial bantering between the scribe and the head judge contin-ues with a double entendre on patriarchal power and the binary male/female gender system:

ESCRIBANO: Luego no es feo delito y mal notado
que un alcalde en persona esté preñado?
BERRUECO: Alcalde siendo, aun mas delito era
siendo fecundo, que hoy esteril fuera?
ESCRIBANO: Necedad es bien rara!
Fecundo quereis sea?
BERRUECO: Pues la vara
á un Alcalde absoluto
de que provecho le es, si no da fruto?

ESCRIBANO: La vara comparais agora al sexo?
BERRUECO: Vos, escribano, no entendeis bien de eso;
una vara concibe dos mil cosas
luego puede parirlas prodigiosas.
Mas haced relacion. (427)

SCRIBE: But isn't it a terrible crime and badly looked on
that a mayor himself be pregnant?
BERRUECO: Being mayor, wouldn't it be a worse crime
that having been fecund, he be today sterile?
SCRIBE: That's a rare stupid idea!
You want him to be fecund?
BERRUECO: The staff
of an all-powerful mayor,
what good is it to him, if it doesn't bear fruit?
SCRIBE: So now you're comparing the staff to the sex?
BERRUECO: You, scribe, don't understand it properly;
a staff can conceive two thousand things
and can later bear them prodigiously.
But summarize your case.

Here, as in the many *entremeses* where Juan Rana plays a mayor, the *vara* or staff is an integral part of his mask. It serves as the theatrical prop to symbolize his mayoral position and status. However, when Berrueco equates the *vara* to the phallus, he identifies it, quite literally, as a quintessential symbol of phallocentric power. The analogy between *vara* and phallus that in other *entremeses* would be considered tentative and covert becomes here a definite and overt double symbol. At the same time, Camilo José Cela indicates that *vara de alcalde* functions as a metaphor for the penis: 'La pija "que manda y gobierna" semeja una vara de alcalde y como tal se comporta' (2:579) (The penis, that governs men's behaviour, looks like a mayor's rod and acts like it too). Accordingly, the *vara* takes on a greater level of symbology affecting the meaning of all of Juan Rana's mayoral *entremeses*. In *El parto*, however, Juan Rana's pregnancy and symbolic *vara* are conceptually combined to form the basis of a debate on power.

While this passage is not overly apparent in its initial questioning tone, it shows that the famous head judge argues in favour of Juan Rana's actions. In Juan Rana's defence, Berrueco exploits both the metaphorical and literal meanings of *dar fruto*. In the metaphorical sense, *Berrueco* applauds the productivity and ability of an all-powerful mayor to give life to many prodigious projects. However, Berrueco would seem to praise Juan Rana's power to bear fruit or, in other words, to reproduce. The head judge also uses the verb *concebir*. In his use of this verb, he belittles the scribe as one who cannot 'conceive' of the power that the symbolic *vara* holds or the many rewarding results that are born from the doings and makings of power. In this way, the pretrial debate on power has in itself turned into a show of power. Quite obviously, Berrueco, as a mayor, is predisposed to side with his professional equal and, as such, puts his inferior, the scribe, in his place.[11]

While Berrueco's power play on words proves him to be sympathetic to Juan Rana's cause, we are, nonetheless, left with a gender conundrum. He has shown that Juan Rana's *vara* symbolizes phallocentric powers but the fact remains that Juan Rana's pregnancy is proof of his female fertility. What is implied here is that Juan Rana's character in *El parto* is a fruitful example of both genders in one or, namely, that his double-sexed condition makes him a hermaphrodite. Gail Bradbury's theory that abnormal sexuality was an integral part of the Spanish *comedia* is thus proven valid. She notes that Baltasar de Victoria includes a commentary on Ovid's tale of *Hermaphroditus* in his 1676 *Del teatro de los dioses de gentilidad* (569):

> Almost inevitably, the overlap between Christian morality and classical culture produced ambivalence and contradiction in seventeenth-century attitudes towards irregular sexuality. Therefore, it is probable that imitations of sexual abnormality on the stage were, although bordering on the improper, rendered less censurable by the precedents in the literature and mythology of the ancients. (577)

This *imitatio* explanation of the depiction of abnormal sexuality and, in particular, the hermaphrodite, would explain that such an *entremés*, perhaps shocking today in some quarters, was common fare in the Spanish Golden Age. In addition, it cannot be forgotten that the *entremés* as a genre was a throwback to the medieval carnival. Notwithstanding, a pregnant Juan Rana implies an act of sexual and metaphorical penetration. Apart from the sodomitical implications, Cameron MacFarlane explains the meaning of this pre-play penetration:

> Within the conventional, masculinist signifying economy, an act of penetrative sexual intercourse is always already gendered. Sex, despite appearances,

always takes place between a masculine, penetrative 'male' and a feminine, penetrated 'female,' and these gendered positions remain absolutely, irrevocably separated. 'Men' penetrate; 'women' are penetrated. For a man '[t]o be penetrated is to abdicate power' (Bersani 252), is to become a woman. (44)

Here the fact that Juan Rana has been penetrated can be seen as a reference to his homosexuality, his abdication of power, and his blurring of the male/female categorization. Berrueco's final words in this passage, *haced relacion*, could be telling the scribe to make the link between *vara*, fecund mayoral productivity, and reproduction. However, the scribe has understood *relación* in a strictly juridical sense, that is, a written or oral statement made to a judge in a trial. His reply shows this to be the case: 'La haré en llegando/ á la junta otros jueces' (427) (I will make it [his statement]/ when the other judges arrive). What can be considered a misunderstanding on the part of the scribe allows the plot to move forward as the other mayors/judges begin to arrive.

With the arrival of the five mayors that will make up the tribunal, the scribe finally has his opportunity to read the charges against Juan Rana:

Primeramente,
el que siendo casado
Juan Rana con Aldonza nunca ha dado
Indicios de ser hombre, pues Aldonza
(al susodicho) siendo una peonza
era quien le mandaba,
le reñia y á veces le pegaba,
logrando en sus contiendas
que él hiciera de casa las haciendas
que barriese, fregase y que pusiese
la olla, y aun á sus mandados fuese. (430)

Firstly,
while being married to Aldonza,
Juan Rana has never given
any indication of being a man, given that Aldonza
(towards the accused) was a shrew,
ordered him about,
scolded him, and on occasion beat him,
succeding through their squabbles

in making him do the household chores,
sweep, mop, wash up, and
see to the meals, and be at her beck and call.

This account details, once again, the well-known fact that Juan Rana is
better suited to being a woman. What is further explained here, however, is the relationship that exists between husband and wife in this
marriage. Indeed, it is the absent Aldonza, Juan Rana's wife, who is the
man of the house ordering about and even beating Juan Rana. She
domineeringly forces Juan Rana to act like a woman in his performance
of household tasks normally considered woman's work. Berrueco, it
would seem, considers Juan Rana's pregnancy to be logical under these
inverted circumstances:

La probanza esta llana
del delito, que imputan a Juan Rana,
del preñado, supuesto
que si el permitió que los cabrones
su mujer se pusiese en ocasiones,
ser el preñado él, no es demasia
pues hizo lo que ella hacer debía. (430)

The evidence against Juan Rana,
in the alleged crime of being pregnant,
is damning, given that,
if he allowed his wife
to wear the balls on occasion,
it's not too inconceivable that he could be the pregnant one,
since he did what she was supposed to do.

In other words, he believes that, if Juan Rana has permitted himself to be
transformed into the woman of the house and marriage bed, then it is
quite logical that he should be the one to carry the child. And as one of
the mayors states, 'La consecuencia es clara,/ mas pues él se lo quiso,
que lo para' (430) (He must face the consequences of his actions/ if
that's the way he wanted it, let him give birth). It would seem that giving
birth, in itself, is a type of punishment for Juan Rana. After some final
deliberations, the tribunal unanimously finds Juan Rana guilty but if, at
the beginning, it seemed that Juan Rana was on trial for his *contra
naturam* condition, it is now clear that he has been found guilty of

allowing himself to be domineered by his wife. His pregnancy is but the visual and growing proof of the extreme to which he has become unmanly. To every crime, of course, there is a corresponding punishment. Berrueco officially announces Juan Rana's long-awaited sentence:

> Decid pues que fallamos,
> debemos condenar y condenamos,
> que á voz de Pregonero,
> que cantando lo expresa al mundo entero,
> que á la vergüenza saquen a Juan Rana
> vestido de mujer (y muy profana)
> donde todos le vean
> y públicos, testigos fieles sean
> de que es su culpa clara
> y si la da allí el parto, que allí para
> y que aquesto mandamos
> que se ejecute luego y no firmamos
> por no saberlo hacer. (431–2)

> We have decided to pronounce sentence,
> we must find him guilty and we have convicted him,
> let our decision be announced by the town crier,
> so that all can hear,
> let Juan Rana be placed on disgraceful display
> dressed as a woman (a shameless hussy)
> so that all may see him,
> and the public bear faithful witness
> to his evident guilt,
> and if he gives birth there, so be it,
> and this we command,
> let it be carried out, and we don't sign
> the order as we don't know how.

It would seem that the judges have decided to out Juan Rana's womanliness, a state usually confined to the home. As punishment he must dress as a woman and be placed on shameful display for all to see. For criminally and unnaturally going against what is considered man's dominant and penetrative nature, an action that has resulted in a 'showing' *contra naturam* condition, Juan Rana is being forced to become a public spectacle and perhaps even to give birth in public. This spectacular and transgendered punishment corresponds, of course, to the theatre production itself, as Marjorie Garber points out:

> The phenomenon of cross-dressing within theatrical representation ... may be not only a commentary on the anxiety of gender roles in modern culture – but also – and perhaps primarily – a back formation: a return to the problem of representation that underlies theater itself. (40)

Significantly, it is stated that he will be dressed in a 'muy profana,' or gaudy, immodest, or even sacrilegious manner. This excessive qualifier, modified by an intensifier, scintillatingly anticipates Juan Rana's grand entrance as an over-the-top, pregnant drag queen. On the other hand, this performance touches on the sacrilegious, which could be seen to underlie Juan Rana's pregnancy. Even within the bounds of this fantastical *entremés*, this pregnancy can be conceived only in terms of a miraculous conception. As such, Juan Rana, in what can be considered a parodic miracle play, would seem to be conceptually linked to the Virgin Birth.

The *enormísimo* and much anticipated arrival of the cross-dressed, pregnant Juan Rana finally comes to pass. As the stage directions indicate, this parodically solemn entrance resembles a miniprocession of sorts: '*Sacan a Juan Rana vestido de mujer y con una barriga muy grande y a Juan Ranilla debajo de las faldas y delante salen el escribano y una mujer cantando en todo de pregón*' (sd 432) (Juan Rana is brought in dressed as a woman with a very large belly and with Juan Ranilla under his skirts. Before them go the scribe and a woman singing at the top of her lungs). This processional entrance also gives weight to the existence of a sacrilegious intent in this *entremés*. We can only imagine the reaction of the audience as they finally get a glimpse of the exaggeratedly large belly of the profanely adorned Juan Rana. In the fashion of a town crier, a woman announces Juan Rana's criminal behaviour and condition:

> Venga á noticia de todos
> como por no ser Juan Rana
> hombre en nada, de mujer
> a la vergüenza le sacan.
> Pues si por el ordinario
> la naturaleza humana
> escribió a Juan Rana antes,

ya le faltaron las cartas.
Sus faltas ha descubierto,
y viendose en nueve faltas,
cuantas palabras pronuncia
son ya palabras preñadas. (432–3)

Let it be known to all that,
for not being a man in any way,
· Juan Rana is being brought out
shamefully as a woman.
If human nature wrote to Juan Rana
regularly in the past,
he's no longer getting the mail.
His faults have been revealed,
and since he has nine of them,
any words he says now
are pregnant words.

This public proclamation substantiates the fact that Juan Rana, in not
being a man in any way, shape, or form, has been dealt by Nature a *contra
naturam* constitution. There is also a series of word associations between
ordinario, faltar, cartas, and *faltas.* As *ordinario* refers to menstruation as
well as regular mail delivery, *faltar las cartas* also means to miss one's
periods. Of course, then, the *cartas* that are missing, the monthly letters
written by nature, are the periods. This analogy is further strengthened
by the subsequent lines, which refer to having gone nine months without
a period, or, having incurred nine *faltas* in the sense explained earlier. In
the two final lines, the words used in this declaration are ironically
considered to be 'impregnated' with truth.

Tried and sentenced in absentia, the forcibly cross-dressed and publicly shamed Juan Rana is allowed to give his side of the story for the first
time. He begins by lamenting his predicament and misfortune:

Ay! desdichada
de quien es su embarazo
su desgracia
y pues no vale, oh! jueces,
razon á la fuerza valga
razon, para que á la fuerza
lo que he concebido, pára. (433)

Oh, miserable wretch
whose predicament is
her disgrace! Reason
is not prevailing, oh judges.
Make reason prevail
so that I may give birth to
what I conceived by force.

Juan Rana's use of *embarazo* refers both literally to his cumbersome pregnancy and metaphorically to his predicament. In this excerpt, however, Juan Rana defends himself against what he sees as an unjust ruling.

Juan Rana continues his plea of innocence in the same section of dialogue:

Valga decir que no sé
si dormiendo ú descuidado
sonando en mí, halle en mi propio
vientre, con mi semejanza.
Valga tambien confesaros
que no soy culpado en nada,
pues este chichon viviente
ningun tropezon le causa. (433)

Let the record show that I do not know
whether while sleeping or daydreaming,
I found my own likeness
in my own belly.
Let it also show that I am
not guilty in the least;
this living bump
doesn't change that.

Juan Rana explains that he does not know how he became pregnant and in the same breath, argues that the 'living bump' is no impediment to his innocence. But at the same time *tropezón* also means 'amorío ilegítiomo' or illicit love affair (Alemán 161 note 91). So basically Juan Rana is saying that the pregnancy is not the result of an illicit love affair, because he, as he goes on to say, must have been ravished without his knowing. His use of *chichon* to describe that which is living within him is also quite significant. *Chichon*, or the swelling that occurs after being violently hit, reminds us that Juan Rana, in the context of this *entremés*, is the victim of spousal abuse. His pregnancy, therefore, can be seen to be the living proof of physical abuse on the part of his wife. When Juan Rana explains that he does not know the origin of his pregnancy and is not guilty of any crime, he is also indicating, through his choice of words, that he is the victim rather than the perpetrator. At the end of Juan Rana's statement one sympathetic mayor is moved to state, 'Su lamento a dolor mueve' (433) (Her lament pains me). His emotional reaction is, however, a comical cue for action.

At this point, Juan Rana exclaims that the climactic moment, both physically and theatrically, has arrived:

> Mas aqui que ha llegado el parto
> Ay! Que se me desencajan
> Las caderas. ¡que dolores,
> Que penas, cielos, que ansias!
> No hay quien me ayude siquiera
> A parir, que muero en tanta
> Fatiga? Mas un temblor
> Me hiela toda, y me pasma.
> Señores, piedad ¡que rota
> Tengo ya la fuente! Que haya
> De parir yo sin comadre
> Habiendo tenido tantas! (433)

> The birth is upon us!
> Ay! My hips are
> dislocating. What pain,
> what grief, heavens, what anguish!
> Isn't there somebody who can help me
> give birth? The effort is
> killing me. I'm trembling,
> an icy chill has come over me, I'm fainting.
> Gentlemen, have pity. My
> fountain has broken! That I should
> have to give birth without midwife,
> having had so many!

In his histrionic and hysterical performance, Juan Rana experiences labour pains and the breaking of his water. In the absence of a midwife, the scribe and two mayors assist. The exclamation, '[Q]ue nos mata!'

(433) (She's going to kill us!), indicates the theatrical and hilarious vehemence of Juan Rana's acting the pregnant part. It is Juan Rana himself, however, who announces the progression and final stage of birth:

Tengan, que del parto está
la cabeza coronada;
mas ya parir con mil diablos;
no me haré otra vez preñada
No mas en mi vida. (433-4)

Hold me down,
the baby is crowning;
after this hellish birth;
I'll never get pregnant again
Never in my life.

In this crowning moment, Juan Rana comically expresses the sentiments of many woman at the moment of birth – never again. While this would seem to indicate that he has learned a lesson from his punishing public ordeal, it cannot be ignored that the staged pregnancy culminates in a parodic birth and makes light of the pain and suffering that women endure in the birthing process.

After a long wait the spectator is rewarded like the pregnant Juan Rana with seeing the joy new life brings. Visually they see a Juan Rana likeness appear: '*Sale por debajo de las faldas Juan Ranilla con sayo*' (sd 434) (A mini Juan Rana in a tunic comes out from underneath Juan Rana's skirts). Berrueco comments on the portraitlike resemblance between the two: 'Su retrato es el muchacho/ en talle y en rostro' (434) (The boy is an exact copy of you/ in figure and face). Here we have, therefore, as in chapter 2, the Juan Rana doubling effect. But if in *El retrato de Juan Rana*, the protagonist adopts the young orphan girl who is his likeness, here Juan Rana has produced his own likeness. Even after giving birth and seemingly after Juan Rana has learned a painful lesson, the gender-bending qualities of his character continue with the first miraculous words of the newborn:

JUAN RANILLA: Mamá
                        No abraza a su Juan Ranilla?
JUAN RANA: Ay! parto de mis entrañas
                        Ay, prenda mia!

ALCALDE PRIMERO: No niega
                   en nada a su padre. (434)

JUAN RANILLA: Mama!
                   Aren't you going to hug your little Juan Rana?
JUAN RANA: Oh, fruit of my loins
                   Oh, my precious!
1ST MAYOR: He looks
                   exactly like his father.

Juan Rana remains double-gendered as both mother and father of a miraculous and immaculately conceived offspring.

Notwithstanding, Juan Rana needs final proof that this is indeed his son:

Aún falta
el saber si es mi hijo, pues
puede ser que otro lo haya
hecho en mi ausencia. (434)

I still
need proof that he's my son,
since someone else might have
made him in my absence.

Juan Rana, already shown to be both father and mother to this child, doubts his own fidelity to himself. To prove his paternity, therefore, Juan Rana puts his son to the test '[v]iendo si es que un zarambeque/ tambien como y le baila' (434) (to see if he can dance a zarambeque, and how well). Juan Rana wants to see if his son can perform a *zarambeque*, the joyful and lively dance that signals the end of an *entremés*. Cleverly, therefore, the ensuing *zarambeque* is thematically used as a test and structurally used to announce the ending of the *entremés*. The accompanying words to the *zarambeque* that Juan Ranilla must dance explain the logic behind his father's test:

Los hijos al padre
En las semejanzas
Como en las mudanzas
Se retratan siempre. (434)

Sons always take after
their fathers in looks
and in the way they move.

In the general sense, these words explain that sons are like their fathers
in their appearance as well as in their actions. In a sense more specific to
Juan Rana's propensity to dance as part of his acting profession, *mudanzas*
also refers to dance moves. Not surprisingly, Juan Ranilla proves he is his
father/mother's son, passing the dancing paternity test with flying colours.

With the playing of another dancing *zarambeque* tune the six mayors
put down their staffs and join in the dance. By joining in the celebration,
the judicial council metaphorically lets go of its phallocentric power.
When the council members let go to rejoice in the birth and proven
paternity of Juan Ranilla, they are, at the same, letting Juan Rana go.
When the scribe asks what they are doing, he receives a revealing answer:

ALCALDE PRIMERO: Querer
                  parecer hoy, de Juan Rana
                  tambien retratos al vivo! (435)

1ST MAYOR: Today
                  we all want to be
                  replicas of Juan Rana.

Caught up in the musical moment, the mayors also want to become lively
portraits of Juan Rana. They too are transformed into multiple Juan
Ranillas. In the end, even the contrary scribe gets into the act:

ALCALDE PRIMERO: Que haceis, escribano?
ESCRIBANO: Ser
                  de Juan Rana semejanza. (435)

2ND MAYOR: What are you doing, scribe?
SCRIBE: I
                  want to be like Juan Rana.

As if by peer pressure, the scribe is also transformed into another Juan
Ranilla likeness. As such, the audience has witnessed an incredible
miracle: the birth of multiple offspring by the hermaphodite, Juan Rana,
and everyone's acceptance of it and him.

At this point, Juan Rana signals the finale of an *entremés*:

TODOS: Pues el natal se celebre
            de Juan Ranilla en Juan Rana.
ESCRIBANO: Conque?
JUAN RANA: Con la conterilla
            conque un entremés se acaba. (435)

ALL: Let Juan Rana's birth of Juan Ranilla
            be celebrated.
SCRIBE: How?
JUAN RANA: With the moral of the story
            That closes an *entremés*.

After the parodic examples within the body of the work, therefore, comes the concluding and concise message of the instructive *entremés*, the *conterilla*. An anonymous female voice sings a moralistic message:

CANTANDO MUJER: Si los hombres parieran
                fuera gran cosa
                pues tuvieran por ciertas
                todas sus obras. (435)

WOMAN SINGING: If men gave birth,
                it would be a great thing
                for they'd know for sure
                that all their works were theirs.

The literal meaning of *parir* is, of course, to give birth. *Obras*, would, therefore, metaphorically refer to women's works, or their children. In this sense, the female voice refers to the traditional idea that a husband can never be sure that he is truly the father of his wife's child. This corresponds to Juan Rana's need to test the paternity of Juan Ranilla. In this way, the text states that if men bore children they would have less anxiety concerning the origin of their offspring. This refers to the perpetual male preoccupation with spousal fidelity and, hence, paternity. Metaphorically, however, *parir*, means to clearly express what one is thinking, and to bring to light what was concealed or unknown. *Obras*, in this case, appears to mean literally men's works in the sense of actions. In this way, the female voice is saying that if men had to give birth to their actions and works as women did their children, men would be more careful and truthful in doing so. The sheer effort involved in giving birth would make them more responsible for their actions and the outcomes of them. This analogy would seem to correspond to Berrueco's initial analogy between *vara*, phallocentric power, and fertility that combined the idea of man's productivity and Juan Rana's unique reproductive abilities.

Although permitted to speak in his own defence only after he was already tried and sentenced, Juan Rana, nonetheless, has the last word, where he agrees with the singing woman's message:

No hay duda, pues que muchas
mujeres vimos
que á mamar á otros padres
los dan los hijos. (435)

That's for sure, because
there are many women who
give their husbands
other men's sons.

Obviously, this is a reference to cheating mothers who lie about the paternity of their sons.

The gender-bending *El parto de Juan Rana* is a commentary on Spanish baroque society as a whole – it is a cry for responsible action on the part of the individual. At the same time, however, it would seem that the patriarchal tribunal in its celebration and symbolic conversion into dancing Juan Ranillas has inadvertently accepted that the ultimate societal construct, the male/female dyad, is a fallacy. As such, *El parto de Juan Rana* celebrates the birth of acceptance, albeit theatrical, of the 'other,' of 'difference.'

La boda de Juan Rana, Juan Rana mujer, and *El parto de Juan Rana* challenge the time-honoured dictum 'clothes make the man.' When Juan Rana crosses the gendered 'clothes'-line, his actions uncover the naked truth that cloaks the strict sex and gender system of Spanish baroque society and of our own – clothes as a 'highly semiotic system' are used as a means to control and oppress. Vestimentary entrapment was particularly oppressive in the case of women and other sexualities. Only in the theatre and more specifically here, in the *entremés*, could a constricting dress code be peeled away to expose and challenge the underlying truth of vestimentary societal constructs.

From a practical standpoint, when a man crosses the gendered 'clothesline,' he is still protected from the elements of nature. This is not the case with the controlling elements that make up society. In the real world, any outward display of inner difference that breaks the existing sex and gender schemas leaves the individual, whether a cross-dressing male, an effeminate male, or a masculine female, unprotected from the open and at times deadly scorn of society. And while Juan Rana was protected from dire straits by his courtly connections, not everyone arrested for the *pecado nefando* or any other infraction of the strict societal codes of the day was so fortunate. While it would seem that Juan Rana was able to shed his second skin on and off the stage, unfortunate others lost the privilege of wearing not only their second skin but also their first, a plight which will be further discussed in chapter 4.

Juan Rana's donning of female apparel is, of course, theatrical and as such, is costume. Outside the realm of theatre, cross-dressing mimics the baroque *mundo al revés* perception of the world and, like the medieval carnival, it challenges the customs of society. As such, onstage cross-dressing aids the audience to envision subversion, the questioning and crossing of societal and self-imposed liminality. It is like a revolutionary light of freedom, albeit temporary and wavering, at the end of the channelling and constricting societal tunnel. Costume challenges customary dress and comportment. It also shows that we are all in 'drag,' all wearing costumes and posturing class, status, sex, and gender. In Juan Rana's case, theatrical costume parodies dress codes and shows us that, like society, clothes can protect us but, at the same time can be our downfall if we step out of bounds. And while clothes, like society, can and do change, societal customs, like fashion trends, are unceasingly redrawn to create restrictive/constrictive limits.

4 'Mas apetezco fuentes que braseros': Phallic Innuendoes and Confessions[1]

In the previous chapters the visual and the semantic can be considered equal partners in yielding the parodic ambiguity desired by Juan Rana and the playwrights who wrote for him. Juan Rana's doubling effect, evident in various physical and artistic forms, operates hand in hand with the many semantic double entendres played on the Juan Rana person and persona. The same can be said of the actor's gender-bending roles as a cross-dressing actor. The theatrical transvestite and the accompanying semantic word plays correlate as a scandalous means of achieving immediate gut-wrenching laughter and a critique of societal identity and perceived reality. The visual effect coexists with the interpretation of puns and word play and vice versa. Each maintained an autonomous ability to induce laughter.

In the *entremeses* studied in this chapter, however, the visual does not possess the capacity to produce laughter independently. The visual becomes comical and, indeed, logical only when semantic double meanings register in the mind of the spectator. Only then does it act as a comedic enhancer. The spectator's understanding of the parodic supersedes his or her seeing of it. This, of course, involves preplay knowledge of Juan Rana's homosexuality and arrest and an active complicity on the part of the listener or reader in understanding contextual references.

The most important treatise of the baroque era on the art of writing drama – Lope de Vega y Carpio's *El arte nuevo de hacer comedias en este tiempo* – includes a noteworthy reference to the fashioning of a complicit spectator.

Siempre el hablar equívoco ha tenido,
y aquella incertidumbre anfibológica,

gran lugar en el vulgo, porque piensa
que él sólo entiende lo que el otro dice. (212)

Ambiguous speech and amphibolic uncertainty
have always been very popular with the masses
because they think that they are the only ones
who understand the joke.

In this passage Lope de Vega precisely states that 'el vulgo' or the lowly
paying public takes great delight in equivocal speech. Of course, equivocal can be interpreted here to mean not only ambiguous but also
dubious and, indeed, sexually lurid. Another important phrase of this
passage is 'incertidumbre anfibológica.' Amphibolic uncertainty or doubt
refers to double meaning and the ambiguity that rises from uncertain
grammatical constructions. This term also denotes the use of ambiguous
phrases and propositions. This most certainly fits the Juan Rana person
and his persona; the amphibious/amphibolic nature implied by the
adopted last name *rana* or frog etymologically linked to duality, ambiguity, and sexual in-betweenness (see chapter 1).

In questions of nature, Lope de Vega would seem to have a keen
understanding of his receptor's psyche. He obviously knew that the
spectator enjoyed not only double meanings but also the act of understanding them and thinking that he or she was the only one in on the
joke. While the baroque theatre public did include a great number of
commoners, it was, nonetheless, a complex audience:

Entre aquel público había mujeres analfabetas, hombres sin ningún género
de estudios, pero todos juntos, con los poetas y los señores que acudían al
espectáculo, tenían la agudeza del pueblo español, su sensibilidad e intui-
ción para adelantarse al ingenio del propio dramaturgo; por ello era nece-
sario que éste 'engañase con la verdad' e hiciese 'hablar equívoco' a sus
personajes dramáticos. (213)

Among the public there were illiterate women, uneducated men, but along
with the poets and gentlemen that attended the show, they possessed the
sharpness of the Spanish people, its sensitivity and intuition to figure out
the genius of the dramaturge himself; for that reason, it was necessary for
him to 'deceive with the truth' and make his dramatic characters prevari-
cate.

Lope de Vega shows that he understands not only the art of writing drama but also the art of pleasing the paying client. Catherine Connor, in her recent study of the spectator as a coproducer of meanings, reinforces Lope de Vega's treatise on audience perception and reception of meaning:

> A sense of catharsis emerges as descriptive within a range of activities involved in trying 'to produce citizen-critics,' and not a prescriptive of how audiences must react to certain art forms (Ford 117). This Aristotelian sense of low pleasures mixed with higher ones helps us understand audiences in their cultural contexts such as in the varied audience of the *corral*, for Aristotle was emphasizing the meanings of pleasures and the pleasures of meanings. (423)

Importantly, it was not only the lowly disempowered *vulgo* who enjoyed the *equívoco*:

> While such meanings could be considered ridiculous or disgusting within elitist aesthetics of dominant minority groups, to the disempowered such productions of meanings can be a source of pleasures of secret resistance and opposition, regardless whether or not such pleasures are ever successful in producing any actual social outcomes of benefit to the popular groups (Barthes, Smith). At the same time, even the elite participated in the grotesque pleasures of popular culture, and their varied pleasures – high and low, as well as in-between or mixed – were possible in the theater semiotics of overlapping and mixed cultural experiences. Their reception is and was diverse, just as might be the carnivelesque laughter and awe provoked by *graciosos*. (424)

Because of the 'high and low, as well as in-between or mixed' makeup of the audience and the polysemic possibilities of meaning, there remained in the mind of many a cultural anxiety towards theatre and its power to educate and, indeed, make the audience think:

> The relationship between elite groups and the majority popular ones in seventeenth-century Spain were contradictory to say the least. Certainly Lope de Vega's theoretical treatise on theater, *Arte nuevo de hacer comedias en nuestro tiempo* and among other *preceptistas* whose treatments he influenced, one finds ... a sense of ambiguity and contradiction regarding popular

audiences and more elite groups (Porqueras and Sánchez). The tensions
surrounding debates among *preceptistas* and moralists about the legitimacy,
morality and the power of public theater, show a fear *and* a celebration of
the spectator's potential for learning and taking pleasure in performances.
(425)

It would seem that the *entremesistas* who wrote specifically for Juan Rana
took to heart and pen Lope de Vega and others' observations and keen
knowledge of the theatrical clientele as well as Aristotle's bodily idea of
cathartic pleasure. Juan Rana's amphibious, ambiguous, and amphibolic
person/persona played an important role in the success of these playwrights and theatre production as a whole.

Hannah E. Bergman signals an important historical note that adds
further fuel to the public's complicit understanding. This critic points
out that many of the *entremeses* apart from being seen on stage were also
meant to be read:

> El lenguaje es la médula de la obra dramática, y para el que la conoce no
> como espectáculo, sino como mera lectura, es el único medio de comunica-
> ción. En el sentido más amplio, pues, toda la comicidad que se puede
> apreciar en una pieza *leída*, es lingüística. (115)

> Language is the centre of drama, and for those who know it not as a show,
> but merely as a work to be read, it is the sole means of communication. In
> the greater sense, therefore, all comicality that can be appreciated in a read
> play, is linguistic.

Indeed, the proliferation of *entremesil* collections in the baroque era is
proof alone of a literate public that enjoyed the written *entremés* in and of
itself: 'Los mercaderes de libros no tardaron en percibir que la afición a
los entremeses era tanta, que se podían vender libros compuestos
exclusivamente de ellos, sin comedias' (25) (The booksellers were quick
to realize that the popularity of *entremeses* was so great, that they could
sell books comprised exclusively of them, without any full-length plays).
Of course, this assumption implies that the reading public had to understand the 'incertidumbre anfibológica' without the aid of visual stimuli.
As readers of complicity they had to understand the semantic double
meanings and implications of the Juan Rana persona without seeing
them.

The semantic double meanings and implications in the *entremeses* of
this chapter specifically concern the *pecado nefando*. The ambiguity of

representation and meaning is based exclusively on Juan Rana's homosexuality and arrest and the knowledge that the public has of both.
While previously, this knowledge was employed as a pretext and subtext
to question identity, reality, the male/female binary construct, and the
oppression of and injustices against women, here homosexual sex acts,
identity, oppression, and persecution take centre stage. Homosexuality
becomes the butt of the joke and the main thrust of the *entremeses*. This
fact represents an extraordinary historical development:

> Conceptualized as the embodiment of a disorder at once sexual, cultural,
> political and religious, the sodomite represented an anarchic force that
> threatened to undermine the nation and against which the nation might
> define itself ... the formation of the sodomite as a social type was to a
> considerable degree the product of a displacement of social crisis, anxiety
> and disruption – a process that figures typically in the construction of the
> 'unnatural' and 'perverse.' (MacFarlane 78–9)

Pedro Calderón de la Barca's *El desafío de Juan Rana* epitomizes the
ongoing moral debate in the baroque era concerning the effeminization
of men, the corresponding fear of homosexualization, and ultimately
the moral, economic, and military weakening of the empire. Here the
playwright, in collusion with Juan Rana, produces a parodic exposé of
the new urban baroque Spanish male seen to be a weakened simulacrum
of the real man. It would seem at least in Calerdón's eyes that the
moralists were fighting a losing battle.

The fencing duel was a sanctioned act of staged violence between
noblemen wishing to avenge offences to their honour. While a public
show of bellicose dexterity, it was, above all, an open performance of
masculinity. However, with the great societal shifts seen during Spain's
baroque period, noble masculinity, as a social construct, was considered
to be in crisis:

> Con la entrada de España a la Modernidad y la formación del Estado, el
> poder político y económico del imperio español se centraliza en la corte y
> en la ciudad urbano-cortesana que deja atrás una cultura medieval de
> carácter rural. Como resultado, la nobleza feudal se urbaniza, perdiendo el
> monopolio del poder militar y desprendiéndose de una masculinidad de
> carácter marcial que ha quedado desfasada. (Cartagena-Calderón 142–3)

> With the entry of Spain into the modern era and the formation of the state,
> the political and economic power of the Spanish empire becomes central-

ized at court and in the urban-courtly city that casts off a medieval, rural culture. As a result, the feudal nobility becomes urbanized, losing its monopoly over military power and discarding a masculinity, military in nature, that has fallen out of favour.

Accordingly, this momentous move to the urban court resulted in a refinement in attire, behaviour, and general demeanour and for many moralists these changes in male behaviour generated ineffective and effeminate men. The general opinion was 'el imperio se había ido irremediablemente a la ruina por haberse presuntamente desvirilizado' (139) (the empire had gone irrevocably to ruin by supposedly having become emasculated). Underlying this perceived lack of masculinity was the primordial fear of the *pecado nefando*, characterized and caricatured as the literary figure of the 'lindo.' José Cartagena-Calderón explains

> que la nueva masculinidad adoptada por los cortesanos se textualiza en la literatura española de la época en la figura caricaturizada del 'lindo,' cuyo afeminamiento los escritores del seiscientos no vacilaron en asociar simbólicamente con la sodomía (homosexualidad). (142)

> that the new masculinity adopted by the courtiers is textually represented in the Spanish literature of the era by the caricaturized figure of the 'lindo,' whose feminization the authors of the 1600s did not hesitate in symbolically associating with sodomy (homosexuality).

> En efecto, el retrato del cortesano 'ahembrado' que adopta una moda femenina y refinada y que tenía a honor el parecer cortés, civilizado y delicado desemboca en la literatura del siglo XVII en la figura caracterizada del 'lindo.' Ya en los inicios del siglo XVII Covarrubias escribe en su *Tesoro de la lengua* (1611), por ejemplo, que '[d]ezir el varón lindo absolutamente es llamarle afemindado' (768), término que define como '[e]l hombre de condición mugeril, inclinado a ocuparse en lo que ellas tratan y hablar su lenguaje y en su tono delicado' (46). La literatura satírica de la época está repleta de diatribas contra los 'lindos,' a quienes, en palabras de José Deleito y Piñuela, se les califica de 'hombres afeminados' y de 'turbia inclinación hacia la gente de su propio sexo' (61). (Cartagena-Calderón 156)

> Effectively, the portrait of the 'effeminate' courtier who adopts a feminine and refined fashion and who placed great importance on appearing courteous, civilized, and delicate, culminated, in seventeenth-century literature, in

the characterized figure of the 'lindo.' Already at the beginning of the seventeenth century, Covarrubias writes in his *Tesoro de la lengua* (1611), for example, that 'calling a male "lindo" is definitively to call him effeminate' (768), a term that he defines as 'womanly man, inclined to interest himself in what women do and speak their language and adopt their delicate tones' (46). The satirical literature of the period is full of diatribes against 'lindos,' who, in the words of José Deleito y Piñuela, are called 'effeminate men' and 'of sordid inclination towards people of their own sex' (61).

However, from early on the Spanish soldier would also seem to be connected to homosexual acts: 'Standard-bearer of empire and man of many pleasures, rogue and hero, the beginnings of the nation and the modern homosexual come together in the representation of queerness in relation to the Spanish military' (Vélez Quiñones 27). As such, within a more urban and military setting, the arms-bearer was well associated with homosexual proclivity. Guido Ruggiero also explains that 'singing, music, (and) fencing ... had become by the mid-fifteenth century threatening rallying points [for a homosexual subculture]' (139). Sherry Velasco highlights this fear as it refers more specifically to baroque Spain:

> Music, dance, spectacle, and popular theater (such as Juan Rana's performance in the interludes) were frequently linked to the feminization of men during the early modern period. Entertainment in general was believed to have softened men and made them useless. Fray José de Jesús María preached in 1600 about the moral and social dangers of theatrical festivities for the masculinity of the male spectator, performer, and participant, arguing that plays are evil, especially erotic dances and the fact that these performances and the concomitant partying made men soft, effeminate, and useless for any difficult or challenging task ... so that they become in a short time so effeminate and cowardly in comparison to how they were once courageous and adventurous (Cotarelo y Mori, *Bibliografía* 375). (184–5)

Taking into consideration the public's knowledge of Juan Rana's irregular sexuality and the resulting duality of his mask, we can see that the actor was a perfect match for Calderón's *El desafío*. Therefore, the *entremés* itself, a site par excellence for singing and music, combined with the illicit sexual overtones of fencing and other symbolic references, makes a strong base for the main homosexual meaning.[2]

Calderón was undoubtedly aware of this great gender and sexual

debate and the general goings-on at court. As such, *El desafío de Juan
Rana* is a parodic representation of a fencing duel that puts into question gender and sexual roles based on well-known homosexual connotations. Adding more fuel to the question of inversion of gender and
sexual roles is Juan Rana's histrionic wife, a strong-minded and virile
woman. Gail Bradbury speaks of the baroque's great interest in irregular
sexuality. More specifically she states, in relation to the era's scientific
study in this field that,

> [i]t would ... be unreasonable to suppose that seventeenth-century drama-
> tists avoided, of necessity, the more sensational aspects of the strong woman/
> weak man topic, or that their audiences were less aware than we are of the
> blurred boundaries between 'inverted' and 'irregular' sexuality. (567)

Bradbury's statement correlates with the relationship that exists between
the weak Juan Rana and his domineering wife in *El desafío* and many
other Juan Rana *entremeses*. Calderón used as a base for *El desafío* a
number of symbols and established clichés concerning homosexuality
and perceived unmanly behaviour, be it on the battlefield, at court, or
on the home front. In addition, Juan Rana and his female cohort further
strengthen the argument for the homosexual reading of Calderón's
jocular *entremés*. On a superficial level, therefore, *El desafío* is a critique of
a demoded test of testosterone practised by noblemen wishing to make
resplendent their tarnished reputation. Evangelina Rodríguez and Antonio Tordera state in the critical edition that '(e)l *entremés* es una parodia
del honor y del duelo o venganza de honor' (200) (the *entremés* is a
parody of honour and the duel or the defense of honour). In a later
work, Rodríguez elaborates on this theme stating that '(e)l antihidalgo
"Juan Rana" desmorona el privilegio de la nobleza de sangre y de la
honra en piezas tan corrosivos como *El desafío de Juan Rana*, conjurando
en la burla ese descrédito del mito en el que comienzan
a participar ecuménicamente engañadores y engañados' (567) (the
antiknight 'Juan Rana' chips away at the privilege of noble blood and of
honour in such corrosive works as *El desafío de Juan Rana*, reinforcing
through mockery this discrediting of the myth, in which both those in
power and those who are not come to participate). This interpretation
of *El desafío* is what can be called the 'straight' take on this *entremés*. This
surface interpretation lacks the full parodic punch that Calderón must
have intended for *El desafío*. Taking into consideration the period's
reevaluation of masculinity, the perceived effeminization of the noble-

man, and the *pecado nefado* panic shown by many moralists, this *entremés* has a more complex and parodic theme. It is a scathing satire of those who bemoan the demise of masculinity and the prevalence of homo-sexuality in a weakened and effeminate noble class. The main objective of this study is to show that Calderón's *entremés* uses the anachronistic duel to critique and satirize the perceived emasculation of the baroque nobleman.

In *El desafío* the offence to the protagonist's honour has taken place prior to the represented dramatic action and, in consequence, the *entremés* consists of retelling this recent offence, preparing for the duel, and showing a partial enactment of the duel itself. In *El desafío*'s first lines, Juan Rana's wife, Bernarda, is surprised by her husband's late arrival for dinner: 'Vos tan tarde a comer? ¡Pierdo el sentido!' (201) (You, late for dinner? I'm stunned!). The humour here lies in the fact that the Juan Rana persona is known to be gluttonous. In this way, the persona's strange behaviour and the ensuing interrogatives by his wife show that something out of the ordinary has happened:

> Decid, ¿qué ha sucedido?
> ¿De qué estáis elevado?
> ¿Esto hacéis a tres meses de casado?
> ¿Descolorido vos y descompuesto? (201)

> Tell me, what has happened?
> What's got you so wound up?
> And this after just three months of marriage?
> Pale and undone?

While his wife's comments can be considered genuine concern for his unhealthy appearance, the fact that the couple has only been married for three months alerts the audiene to the first thing normally associated with newlyweds in popular culture, sex. Indeed, the use of 'elevado' (literally, lifted up) would seem to have a sexual reference. In this way Bernarda acts the part of a newlywed who suspects her husband of infidelity and would seem to have the proof before her eyes. Juan Rana's subsequent reply brings up the question of honour and the fact that he does not have a clear conscience (202). This would seem to refer to a compromising sexual encounter on the part of the tardy, pale, and 'undone' newlywed Juan Rana, uncustomarily late for dinner. In addi-tion to this guilt-ridden comment, there is a series of sexual references that question not only Juan Rana's marital relationship but also his sexuality. This weak man/strong woman marriage between Juan Rana and his wife epitomizes what was discussed in the opening pages of chapter 3 (65–71). Especially important here are Susan C. Shapiro's and Cameron MacFarlane's comments on the effeminate male who on one level denotes homosexuality but at the same time, the loss of patriarchal and penetrative male power.

Juan Rana explains to his wife that he needs 'un manto' (202) so as to 'reñir de medio ojo' (202) with a friend or, in other words, he needs a cape to take part in a duel in a covert manner. With regard to *de medio ojo* Rodríguez and Tordera explain that it means to do something in hiding, as must have been the case with duels, which were prohibited. For this reason, he asks for a *manto*, a feminine article of clothing (202 note 16). While they mention that the *manto* is specifically a 'prenda feminina,' they make no reference to a possible gender inversion. The need for Juan Rana to appear incognito underlines the secrecy of the duel. But at the same time, the need to camouflage one's activities is a covert reference to the clandestine nature of illicit sexual encounters. It is interesting to note that on speaking about the inherent nature of skirmishes Juan Rana utters: '¿No *veis* que el más amigo es quien la pega?' (202) (Don't you see that it's your best friend who betrays you?). On one level of interpretation Juan Rana declares that friends are the first to betray you, but *ser de la pega* is also a phrase used for a person who forms part of a group of men who live a life of vice and scandal. This would seem to make reference to Juan Rana's dubious behaviour in the company of other men.

The following dialogue would also seem to indicate that Juan Rana's marriage of three months is by no means blissful:

JUAN: Pues yo, aunque no te alabo,
           de lo que tengo en vos ... estoy al cabo.
BERNARDA: Sé que podéis decir con mil placeres,
           que en mí tenéis un molde de mujeres.
JUAN: Esos son ... los hechizos:
           que diz que me ponéis algunos rizos. (202)

JUAN: Well, although I don't brag about you,
           I know what a prize I have in you.
BERNARDA: I know you can happily say,
           that in me you have a paragon of a woman.
JUAN: It's the magic spells:
           People say that you make my hair curl.

Another meaning of *estoy al cabo* is to be on one's last breath. In this sense, Juan Rana is saying that he is exasperated with his wife and this after such a short period of marriage. Rodríguez and Tordera give an additional interpretation of the phrase, saying that here Calderón is extending the metaphor of illness that Bernarda just used to express her impatience with her husband's reticence to explain his actions: 'De esperallo estoy con tabardillo' (202) (I'm dying to find out). While *estar con tabardillo* as well as *estar al cabo* refer to grave illness, *tabardillo* can also refer to a predominantly male garment, the *tabardo*, or smock. This creates an additional link between Juan Rana's *manto*, a female garment, mentioned a few lines earlier, and Bernarda's tabardo, a male garment – yet another example of gender inversion. To her comment that she is an ideal woman, a 'molde de mujeres,' Juan Rana replies that she is actually a witch. Her witchcraft is such that she has curled his hair. Would this be the result of the fear he holds of her feminine powers? Notwithstanding this possible interpretation, the accompanying phrase 'ponerse algunos rizos' easily lends itself as a euphemism for *ponerle los cuernos* (to cuckold), thus implying her infidelity. In this way, this series of double meanings culminates in the ultimate insult to the male ego, the cuckolded husband.

However, the 'rizos' allusion quickly changes meaning in Bernarda's reply:

¿Rizos a vos, esposo?
No lo habéis menester, que sois hermoso.
¡Qué cintura tenéis! *Toma* un(a) higa. (202–3)

Curl your hair, husband?
You don't need it, you're handsome.
What a figure you have! I salute you.

'Rizos' seems to preserve here its more literal meaning of curls but Juan Rana adorned with real curls combined with Bernarda's ironic comments on his wonderful figure and her calling him handsome makes for a reversal of roles, indicating that he is a 'lindo' and insinuating the other sexuality. This reference to *rizos* is a significant homosexual reference:

Recordemos ... que en la España de la temprana Edad Moderna, los hombres que habían sido encontrados culpables de prácticas homosexuales eran llevados a la hoguera, 'realizando un último paseo en el que el condenado era mostrado trasvestido y con el pelo rizado' (Rossi 61). Como indica, por su parte, Martín, 'In Spain artificially curled hair was emblematically linked with effeminacy and homosexuality (and by extension the crime of sodomy) by the Inquisition, the institution generally responsible for punishing the latter' ('Rereading El amante liberal' 156). De ahí que los rizos de los cortesanos hayan levantado las más feroces críticas de tradistas como Castiglione, Della Casa y Gracián Dantisco, quienes se vieron obliga-dos a tomar medidas contra el peligroso afeminamiento de los cortesanos, no sólo por sus caras delicadas y su ropajes femininos, sino, porque 'se encrespan los cabellos,' como dice Castiglione (97). (Cartagena-Calderón 159–60)

We must remember that in the Spain of the early modern age, men found guilty of homosexual practices were sent to the gallows, 'paraded there dressed in women's clothing and with their hair curled' (Rossi 61). As Martín also indicates ... This is why courtiers' curls were fiercely criticized by moralists like Castiglione, Della Casa, and Gracián Dantisco, who felt it necessary to take action against the dangerous feminization of the courtiers, not only for their delicate faces and feminine robes, but also because they 'curled their hair,' as Castiglione states.

Apart from this homosexual reference, the husband is also mockingly objectified through his wife's gaze, as the 'toma un(a) higa' would imply. Rodríguez and Tordera, citing from the *Diccionario de Autoridades*, ex-plain that *tomar una higa* is used to praise someone's beauty through flattery. However, Cela gives an alternative vulgar definition of *higa* and its variants that fills nine pages (1:225–34). He indicates that a 'showing someone the finger' meaning of *higa* was used in *La Celestina* (228), *Don Quijote* I/II (228–9), and *La loçana andaluza* (230), and goes back not only as far as ancient Rome, but even as far as the Old Testament. This suggestive phrase with its accompanying gesture was, therefore, well known by the baroque audience. As such, the protagonist is presented as a powerless and ultimately effeminate man. In addition, Juan Rana proclaims: 'Yo sé que soy galán, Dios me bendiga./ Pero dan en decir, que es lo que siento,/ que os parezco mejor cuando me ausento' (203) (I know I am a gallant, God help me./ But they hurt me when they say, and I feel it, too,/ that you like me better when I am absent). There is a semantic connection between *galán* and *marión*, the latter a well-known period euphemism for effeminate man/homosexual (Thompson 'Juan Rana: A Gay Golden Age *Gracioso*' 245). In this way, Juan Rana would seem to be admitting his homosexuality. It is no surprise, then, that Juan Rana's wife should cheat on him and be happier when he is absent (203).

At this point in the *entremés* Juan Rana gives a general description of the preplay insult to his honour. Significantly, the inverted sexuality hinted at up to this point in the *entremés* takes centre stage in the following dialogue:

BERNARDA: ¿Vos molido? ¿Con qué?
JUAN: Con un garrote.
          ¿No conocéis, mujer, a Gil Parrado?
          Pues tras haberme con un garrote dado,
          Sólo porque yo so vuestro marido,
          me dijo ...
BERNARDA: ¿Qué cosa decid?
JUAN: Que era sofrido.
BERNARDA: Que érais sufrido os dijo en mi perjuicio (203 ll.38–43)

BERNARDA: You, beaten up? With what?
JUAN: With a club.
          Don't you know Gil Parrado?
          Well, he gave it to me with a big club,
          Only because I'm your husband,
          he said ...
BERNARDA: What did he say?
JUAN: That I'm walked all over.
BERNARDA: That insult was directed at me.

Taking into consideration the gay text of *El desafío*, the sexual references that have emerged up to this point in the *entremés*, and the imagery used here, Juan Rana's explanation must also be read on a level other than that of the simple thrashing of a husband who silently endures his wife's inappropriate behaviour. *Garrote*, or club, is an explicit phallic symbol and *dar*, or to give, is an obvious sexual reference. In the sense of *golpear*, or to hit, it belongs to the 'vocabulario bélico de las "batallas de amor"' (Alzieu et al. 126 poem 73, note 1) (the bellicose vocabulary of 'love's battles'). We have, therefore, an encoded description of an act of buggery performed on our *passim* protagonist. These sodomitic double meanings continue in the ensuing exchange between husband and wife:

BERNARDA: ¿Con palo os dio que la honra tanto daña?
JUAN: En fin, gracias a Dios, no fue con caña.
BERNARDA: En fin, tontón, menguado,
            que a mis ojos venís apaleado.
JUAN: Cierto que la memoria tengo flaca,
            Pues no sé si era palo o [...] era estaca. (203)

BERNARDA: He gave it to you with a stick so badly that it hurt your honour?
JUAN: At least, God be thanked, it wasn't with a cane.
BERNARDA: And so, fool, coward,
            you come beaten into my sight.
JUAN: .   I have a short memory,
            I don't know if it was a stick or a stake.

The wife's question strengthens the argument for a buggery interpretation. Indeed, what rod if not a metaphorical erect penis could hurt so much one's honour? Cleverly, the verb *apalear*, or to hit with a stick, takes on a new homoerotic connotation, and *estaca*, a yet larger *palo*, shows the augmentative value of this metaphor and surely of the spectator's laughter. This also gives other connotations to the words *dolencia*, *penas*, *daña*, *sufrido*, and *molido* that pepper the text. Rodríguez, in a discussion of theatrical iconography, notes that

[a]lgunos dibujos de comienzos del siglo XIII ... refuerzan esta visión negativa de la actividad teatral, pues los actores, al estilo de los mimos romanos o de los posteriores polichenelas renacentistas, se manifiestan en ingrávidas actitudes ridículas, llevando bastones o palos (como el gracioso carnavalesco español portará el matapecados) o insinuando la obscenidad de un prominente falo. (48)

[s]ome drawings from the beginning of the thirteenth century ... reinforce this negative view of theatre activity, given that the actors, in the style of Roman mimes, or like the rump of the Commedia dell'Arte character Polichinela, are shown in ridiculous and gravity-defying positions, carrying canes or sticks (like the carnivalesque Spanish buffoon would carry a staff) or insinuating the obscenity of an erect phallus.

Quite obviously, a hand-held cylindrical object has a long history of phallic symbology.

With the explanation of the offensive event complete, it is Juan Rana's wife who urges him to write 'un papel de desafío' or an invitation to a duel (204) to which our protagonist replies: '¡De vos me admiro!/ Yo en el campo con nadie no me tiro' (204) (You amaze me!/ On the field I won't draw for anyone). Apart from the obvious reversal of male/female roles and Juan Rana's cowardly conduct, the place where the protagonist is unable to *tirarse* is on one level *el campo de batalla* (the battlefield) but another, if we continue with the sexual interpretations, connotes *el campo de batalla sexual*. Brian Dutton has shown how in a poem in the *Cancionero de San Roman*, the *campo de batalla* actually becomes a bed where the fencers fornicate: 'mas el bien de nuestro lecho/ es un campo de contrafecho' (our bed/ is a field of contravention).[3] His finding reinforces the *campo-lecho* (field-bed) connection in Calderón's *entremés*. It must also be remembered that many illicit sexual encounters took place out of doors, metaphorically mirroring the fact that they were outside the rules of accepted society.

The reversal of gender roles continues with Juan Rana's wife instructing her husband on how to fence but, once again, there is a different type of coaching going on:

BERNARDA: Mirad, marido, cuanto a lo primero,
os habéis de calar bien el sombrero,
sacar la espada con gentil despecho,
entrar el pie derecho,
poneros recto, firme y perfilado. (204)

BERNARDA: Look, husband, the first thing you have to do
is adjust your hat,
unsheath your sword with noble disdain,
put your right foot forward,
stand erect, firm, and tall.

Here for the first time the word *espada* appears in the text although the *desafío* or duel in the play's title makes implicit reference to the use of swords. In other words, the metaphorical sword is always hanging over the spectator's head. In this revealing passage, *espada*, apart from its bellicose definition, quite obviously and graphically describes a penis that is 'recto, firme y perfilado.' Traditionally, the sword symbolizes the erect phallus. More specifically during the Spanish Golden Age, weapons of all kinds acquired a phallic interpretation. Brian Dutton has shown in the same *Cancionero de San Roman* poem mentioned above how there are explicit references to the lance as phallus and John T. Cull has written on the phallic symbolism of Don Quijote's broken lance (40–2). In the case of *El desafío*, fornication is covertly implied under the guise of swordplay with a homoerotic/parodic twist. In this way, the seemingly unassuming dueling title in itself refers, on a second level, to the phallus and in general terms to *luchar/ lucha*, a euphemism for having sex (Alzieu et al. 11, poem 5, l. 4; 44, poem 28, l. 7). Consequently, this first use of *espada* in the text brings together fencing and fornication and, in doing so, connects the host of phallic symbols used previously and gives a particularly poignant second meaning to the *entremés*'s title.

Moreover, Juan Rana's reply hints at not only his cowardice, but also his unmanliness:

¿ ... ponerme recto, firme y afilado,
entrar con tiento y ¡zas¡ darle una herida?
¿Es más? Pues esto no lo erré en mi vida. (204)

... stand erect, firm and sharp?
enter with a steady hand and bang! give him a wound?
What more? I'd never do that in my life.

It would seem that the emasculated Juan Rana implies that he is unable to be the active partner in the sexual act.[4] The collection of erotic poetry by Pierre Alzieu et al. includes a poem that ridicules a *caballero* unable to raise his euphemistic sword in a *batalla sexual* with a *dama* (242, poem 122, note to l. 14). This would seem to parallel Juan Rana's inability, be it physical or physiological, to firmly raise his sword and strike his mark. In accordance with a long-standing Mediterranean tradition and in the eyes of the Inquisition, the *passive* partner was considered more *contra naturam* and less masculine than his active cohort and was more seriously punished for this reason: 'Tradicionalmente el sodomita activo ha sido considerado como "macho" y el pasivo como "hembra," y el pueblo reserva su mayor desprecio para el femenino' (Pérez Escochotado 178) (Traditionally, the active sodomite has been considered 'male' and the passive 'female,' and people have more disdain for the feminine partner). Therefore, Juan Rana is not only portrayed as a sodomite but also as the lowly and viler passive partner in male buggery.

Finally, after a series of comic deliberations, the *papel de desfío* is drawn up and made ready to be sent. Only at this moment does the Juan Rana mask truly realize that the duel will take place. Crying in his customary cowardly and unmanly manner, Juan Rana's words of wisdom to his wife reveal her questionable sexual past:

> y que miréis por Juanico
> que en fin, so su padre, puesto
> que a tres meses de casado
> me nació en casa de tiempo
> y adiós que no puedo más. (207–8)

> and watch over Juanico
> for after all, I am his father, since
> after three months of marriage
> he was born at home at full term
> and farewell – I can't take any more

Be it through ignorance, gullibility, or both, the laughable Juan Rana believes that the son born to his wife three months after marriage is his. It would seem, therefore, that his wife rumoured to be unfaithful or *de haberle puesto algunos rizos* was equally unchaste before their marriage. In this way the weak, cowardly, dense, gullible, cuckolded, and effeminate Juan Rana isn't even the father of his wife's son.

Subsequently, Bernarda insults him for his negative and unmanly traits and quickly vanishes to send the *papel de desafío*. Officiously, the infamous Gil Parrado immediately appears on stage with the note in his hand. The resulting combative dialogue between Juan Rana and his sparring partner is once again quite revealing. As if offended for receiving such a hateful document, Gil Parrado asks: '¿Cómo tiene atrevimiento/ de desafiarme a mí?' (209) (How dare you have the nerve/ to challenge *me*?). With this sudden appearance, Juan Rana exclaims in an aside to the public, that Gil Parrado '(c)ogióme/ entre puertas. Esto es hecho' (209) (trapped me. / It's a fact). This direct comment to the public adds a level of complicity between Juan Rana and the public. It is as if the public becomes Juan Rana's confidant and as such becomes drawn into the play as Juan Rana's complicit sidekick. On an idiomatic level, *cogerme entre puertas* means to corner someone with no means of escape and, using violence, force him to do what is desired. This idiomatic expression that speaks of entrapment and violent obligation combined with the prior evidence of the homoerotic would suggest that the other colloquial and sexual meaning of the verb *coger* is insinuated here (Alzieu et al. 25, poem 15, l. 1; 268, poem 134, l. 7), namely that Gil Parrado has forced him to engage in sex. In this sense, we now have the first specific reference to Juan Rana's preplay offence, a homosexual act of the recent past.

The ensuing exchange between the two fencers adds further homoerotic double meaning to the text. To try to explain the reason behind sending the offensive *papel de desfío*, Juan Rana seems to make up a story:

> JUAN: Cierta opilación que tengo
>   fue la causa.
> GIL: ¿Como ansí?
> JUAN: Hanme dado por remedio
>   que haga ejercicio y que riña
>   para tomar el acero.
> GIL: Sígame
> JUAN: ¿Dónde me lleva?
> GIL: Al campo. (209)

> JUAN: A certain blockage
>   was the cause.
> GIL: What?
> JUAN: As a remedy they told me to
>   exercise and fence
>   in order to take iron.
> GIL: Follow me.
> JUAN: Where are you taking me?
> GIL: To the field.

As Rodríguez and Tordera have noted in their edition

> [s]e juega con el doble sentido de empuñar la espada y del remedio que se da a los que padecen de opilación. La terapéutica especial de esta enfermedad (obstrucción de los conductos humorales) consistía en 'tomar el acero,' lo cual ... podía hacerse o saliendo al campo muy de mañana o bien tomando agua ferruginosa. (209 note 163)[5]

> [t]here is a play on the double meaning of *empuñar la espada* and the remedy given to those who suffer from humoural blockages. The particular therapy for this illness consisted in 'taking steel,' which could be done either by going for early-morning strolls in the country or by taking iron-rich water.

In this case, Juan Rana has taken 'tomar el acero' to mean 'empuñar la espada,' to bare steel, and, as such, the remedy for his illness is the euphemistic fencing duel. While this double meaning in itself adds an element of humour to the text, there is an additional and less innocent double meaning of *reñir para tomar el acero*.

Camilo José Cela explains that *acero* is a poetic euphemism that is clearly used to signal the penis, which has the temper of steel (2:255). In a more historical and literary context, Alzieu explains that *acero* means phallus and that its use as remedy for curing *opilación* was a well-known joke in the Golden Age. Indeed, this well-known joke is precisely the subject of a comedy by Lope de Vega (*El acero de Madrid*) (Alzieu et al. 178 poem 93, note to l. 45). In the same note, Alzieu et al. includes a *letrilla* by Luis Góngora y Argote that graphically shows a metaphorical correlation between the medicinal and sexual meaning of *dar el acero* as a remedy for *opilación*:

Opilóse vuestra hermana
y diola el Doctor su acero;
tráela de otero en otero
menos honesta y más sana:
diola por Septiembre el mana,
y vino a purgar por Mayo.

Your sister was suffering a blockage
and the doctor gave her his steel;
he takes her over hill and dale
she's less honest but more healthy;
in September he gave her a purgative
and she purged in May.

Indeed, in Góngora's less than euphemistic use of *dar* (to fornicate), *acero* (the phallus), *mana* (semen), and *purgar* (to give birth) – in this case, nine months after the 'cure' – the sexual meaning of the Juan Rana text becomes quite blushingly obvious. In the case of *El desafío*, however, Juan Rana takes (*tomar*) rather than gives (*dar*), which underlines that the protagonist is the *passim* partner in his past act of buggery as we have already seen. In this way, Calderón uses a well-known topos employed by Lope de Vega and Góngora that describes a sexual remedy for humoural blockages as the foundation of the homoerotic humour in this passage.

As *El desafío* draws to a close, there is another reference to food, in this instance a *merienda*, or an afternoon snack. As we recall, the *entremés* started with the uncustomary late arrival of Juan Rana for dinner. Thematically, therefore, this *entremés* gastronomically comes full circle. But if, at the beginning of the *entremés*, there was only a hint of sexual impropriety with Juan Rana's absence for dinner, the future *merienda* between the fencers holds much food for sexual thought:

> JUAN: Voy al momento
> a prevenir la merienda.
> GIL: Yo sólo a reñir le llevo.
> JUAN: Es que ando buscando trazas
> para matarle comiendo,
> y ha de ser con un bocado.
> GIL: Gracioso está. Saque presto
> la espada y tire a matarme.
> JUAN: Usted piensa que es buñuelo.
> Espérese, que según
> mi mujer, he de entrar presto,
> y de echalle cierto atajo. (208–9)[6]

> JUAN: I'll pack a picnic.
> GIL: I'm only taking you to fight.
> JUAN: It's just that I've been thinking of
> ways to kill you while you eat
> and it must be by poison.
> GIL: You're funny. Draw your sword
> this instant and strike to kill.
> JUAN: You think this is going to be easy.
> Wait just a minute; my wife
> says I should move quickly
> and parry a bit.

While on the surface, this would seem to be merely a comical exchange between duelists, it has another meaning. *Bocado* is a euphemism for the penis (Cela 2:282) as well as a mouthful of something; the metaphorically phallic sword now makes its second appearance, and the verbs *entrar* (to enter) and *echar* (to discharge), both heavy with sexual meaning, are used. In this way, we may conclude that the *merienda* does not specifically involve eating food. In this way, the verb *reñir*, used throughout the text, can be seen to have a sexual connotation that is connected to its synonym *luchar,* a verb we have shown to be a sexual euphemism for fornication.

Finally, the much-anticipated duel takes place but, ironically, it is of short duration as the highly amusing skirmish begins and ends in seven lines of dialogue (211) and is of little combative significance. Juan Rana strikes his partner with a slipper and Parrado cries for help in fear for his life. Obviously, by traditional standards, neither Parrado nor Juan Rana exemplify the baroque macho male. On the contrary, in their childish spat, they represent two *lindos* and while the sexual connotations that prevailed in the rest of the *entremés* are now absent, the cowardly and unmanly actions of the duelists speak for themselves. Ultimately, the performance of the protagonists combined with the length and ridiculous nature of this confrontation show that the duel was but a pretext for the true intention of *El desafío,* to satirize the obsession with masculinity versus effeminization during the baroque period.

Hearing Parrado's cry, the police immediately arrive, staying the duel. In theatrical terms, therefore, the metatheatrical duel climaxes too early and sexually the sparring partners do not complete their duel, unreservedly implying their lack of virility. But Juan Rana, with much false bravado, speaks of his fearlessness in many past duels and, as such, puts on a virile front. This sentiment quickly dissipates when Juan Rana learns that he is to be taken off to prison. In the nick of time, however, Bernarda arrives to save him from this fate. As is the *entremesil* custom, *El desafío* has a moralizing finale.

> BERNARDA: Por valiente a Juan Rana
> prenderle quieren.
> JUAN RANA: Eso es lo que se saca
> de ser valientes.
> BERNARDA: Ya es valiente Juan Rana
> ténganle miedo.
> JUAN RANA: Para cuando las ranas
> tengan más pelo. (212–13)

> BERNARDA: They want to arrest Juan Rana
> for being a gallant.
> JUAN RANA: That's what you get
> for being a gallant.
> BERNARDA: Juan Rana is a gallant;
> fear him.
> JUAN RANA: When pigs fly.

This traditional and moralizing ending serves as a metatheatrical wrap-up of the *entremés*. As such the actors slip out of one character, to take on another. In their more moralistic roles, they direct themselves towards the public. In doing so, the audience is given the impression that the actors are out of character, but of course this is not the case; they have only taken on other traits and another level of playful reality.

In this other-stage reality wrap-up, the word *valiente* is used three times, but it is unclear whether it is used as an adjective or a noun. As an adjective, *valiente* refers to superior lineage, exemplary valour, and physical and moral fortitude, positive traits that constitute the traditional social construct of noble masculinity. As a noun, *valiente* is the equivalent of *valentón* or *baladrón*, a braggart. This last, negative connotation is quite fitting for the Juan Rana character in *El desafío*. Juan Rana speaks disapprovingly of the whole *valiente* business and seems to imply that prison would be a just punishment. In his last lines and those of the *entremés*, he refers to the extreme improbability of people fearing him for being *valiente*, which is tantamount to openly declaring that he is not and never will be *valiente*.

Unmistakably, the symbolic connection between fencing, the phallus and fornication is well entrenched in the parodic *El desafío de Juan Rana*. This connotative connection allows Calderón to make light of the baroque preoccupation with the effeminization of the male construct. In this way, *El desafío* is an effective satire of noblemen and the social constructs that bind them. Evidently, the Spanish baroque theatre relished the homosexual double entendres, as *El desafío de Juan Rana* shows. Nevertheless, the use of homosexual references can be seen as laughter at the expense of the disenfranchised other. The homosexual, one of the most hated and persecuted minorities in history, is considered fair game for mockery and worse still.

El sodomita es vil, despreciable, abominable. Despúes del hereje, es el criminal más detestable que se puede encontrar, más criminal e infame que el regicida o el parricida, más que el traidor. El sodomita es infame en cualquier contexto institucional o jurídico que se aprecie. Que sea religioso, noble, militar, procurador en Cortes en ejercicio, etc., pierde toda inmunidad, todo privilegio, todo fuero. (Carrasco 21–2)

The sodomite is vile, despicable, abominable. After the heretic, he is the most detestable criminal that is to be found, more criminal and dishonourable than those found guilty of regicide or patricide, more than the traitor.

The sodomite is dishonourable in any possible institutional or juridic context. Whether he is a clergyman, a noble, a soldier, a lawyer, etc., he loses all immunity, all standing, all privilege.

As such, Juan Rana is presented stereotypically as a gullible, henpecked, weak, cowardly, cuckolded, and ultimately laughable man. While presenting a stereotypical image of the *lindo* or homosexual, however, the overriding moral tenor of the *entremés* rejects and ridicules the unrealistic *valiente* traits of manliness, the other extreme of masculinity. Accordingly, this theatrical and comic depiction of homosexuality is a testimony of its prevalence and power to fuel the imagination. Perhaps, in the end, the best medicine against repression and hatred is to face the oppressor on his or her terms as Juan Rana did throughout his successful and long theatrical career as a *gracioso*.

Considering the visual and symbolic potency of the sword and swordplay, it is not surprising that other *entremesistas* of the period used this poignant and pointed metaphor when writing for Juan Rana. In Luis Quiñones de Benavente's *Los muertos vivos*, this time-honoured phallic metaphor once again raises its head. This *entremés* was included in Quiñones de Benavente's celebrated *Joco Seria* posthumously published in 1653.[7] This playwright has been called 'el mas ingenioso, fecundo y discreto de nuestros festivos entremesistas' (La Barrera y Leirado 31) (the most gifted, prolific, and eloquent of our festive *entremesistas*). Hannah E. Bergman considers him to be the Lope de Vega of minor theatre (9) and the most highly regarded *entremesista* of his time (41). While these accolades may be true, Bergman's comments on the work of Quiñones de Benavente would seem to present a false impression: 'Domina en ella una sátira moral siempre suave, más certera, condenando los vicios no en lo abstracto y terrorífico, sino en sus aspectos humildes y cotidianos' (9) (His work is dominated by a gentle and just moral satire, condemning vice not abstractly and terrifyingly, but in its humble, daily aspects). At times, Bergman's passion for Quiñones de Benavente's work would seem to hinder her from lending a more critical eye to what may be considered a more below the belt/between the lines analysis of the jocose elements in Quiñones de Benavente's work. She states:

Con plena comprensión de este principio didáctico, dado por la naturaleza con un finísimo sentido de lo cómico y una ingeniosidad incansable, dueño de un vocabulario castizo pero rico en giros populares, con una maestría en la métrica pocas veces igualada, Luis de Benavente supo granjearse los aplausos de sabios e ignorantes sin abandonar jámas su alto propósito moral.' (74).

Luis de Benavente, who had a full understanding of this didactic principle, who was gifted by nature with a highly refined sense of the comic and an inexhaustible inventiveness, who was master of a learned vocabulary none-theless rich in popular sayings, and who enjoyed an almost unequalled mastery of metre, knew how to win the applause of the educated and the uneducated alike without ever abandoning his lofty moral purpose.

Her important study does, nonetheless, provide key historical informa-tion surrounding the production of the *entremeses* and many points of departure for a more risqué analysis of the Juan Rana *entremeses* written by Quiñones de Benavente. As will be seen in the analysis of the *Los muertos vivos*, Quiñones de Benavente's moral satire was not always *suave* nor was it per se habitually condemnatory.

Los muertos vivos centres on Juan Rana's refusal to allow his sister to wed. As a result, his sister and her fiancé Juan Pérez play a vindictive trick on the protagonist. Bergman cites historical data concerning this *entremés*, explaining who is who in the dramatis personae, and more importantly, dating the production of this *entremés* to 1636, the same year as Juan Rana's arrest for the *pecado nefando*.

After the initial swordplay between Juan Rana and Juan Pérez, his prospective brother-in-law, the sister with the aid of her suitor tricks the protagonist into believing that he is dead. What ensues is a series of comical situations where the 'dead' Juan Rana does not 'act' as a corpse. He converses with his sister and sits up on his deathbed, causing his many visitors to flee in fear. At one point, Juan Pérez continues the trick by becoming a false corpse. With the arrival of another actor dressed as the devil, both 'corpses' race around the stage fleeing from their satanic perpetrator (222). When the demonic mask is removed, the brother and future brother-in-law make peace after their deathly encounter with the devil. This parodic simulacrum of death and a 'devilish' meeting comes to its moralistic end with a wish that the spectators 'rianse de aqueste por amor de Dios' (233) (fully enjoy the *entremés*). The initial swordplay skirmish between Juan Rana and the future brother-in-law is, however, the main area of interest to this study.

In great contrast to Calderón's delayed mention of the *espada* in *El desafío de Juan Rana*, Quiñones de Benavente physically places the sword in the hands of Juan Pérez from the onset of the action as the stage directions indicate: '*Sale Juan Pérez con la espada desnuda atras Cosme* (Juan Rana)' (225) (Juan Pérez comes onstage, his sword drawn, chasing after Cosme). Considering Juan Rana's arrest for the *pecado nefando* in 1636 – the same year that the *entremés* was produced – and the phallic implications of the sword and swordplay that we have seen, it would appear that his recent 'criminal' past is figuratively pursuing him on-stage. The 'naked' sword held behind him by his pursuing partner can be considered a *pecado nefando* analogy from the onset of the *entremés*.

Once again the stage directions are quite revealing. They indicate physical proximity and repositioning: '*Hincase Cosme* [Juan Rana] *de rodillas y Juan* [Pérez] *alça la espada*' (226). At this point it would seem that Juan Rana is kneeling in front of Pérez who has raised high the symbolic sword in the manner of Abraham, about to sacrifice his only son, as Ignacio Arellano et al have noted in their edition of *Jocoseria* (655 note 13). What is at first an obvious physical threat quickly changes into a sexual one:

PÉREZ: Vive Christo, que os mate.
JUAN RANA: Abraham, tate, tate.
PÉREZ: Yo os quiero hablar sin colera.
JUAN RANA: Y yo quiero,
             recule un poco atras, como cochero
PÉREZ: Juan Rana, el mas bonito que yo he visto.

[*Pérez*] *Va tras el y suelta la espada, y el* [*Juan Rana*] *huye.* (226)

PÉREZ: For the love of God, I'll kill you.
JUAN RANA: Stop, stop, you Abraham!
PÉREZ: I want to talk to you calmly.
JUAN RANA: And I want you
             to back up a bit, like a coachman
PÉREZ: Juan Rana, the cutest one I've seen.

[*Pérez*] *goes after him and drops the sword, and he* [*Juan Rana*] *flees.*

When Juan Rana states that he wants Pérez to back up like a coachman, he would seem to indicate that he wishes to be distanced from the physical threat of the sword. It would seem, however, that Juan Pérez has taken his statement to mean something entirely different. Juan Pérez states that Juan Rana is cute and makes for him, dropping the sword and possibly positioning himself behind the protagonist. Here the metaphorical sword of flesh becomes the threatening weapon. Juan Rana, recently arrested for what must have been a similar physical and compromising position, ironically flees this onstage reenactment of his 'crime.'

The ensuing dialogue between the two actors fighting for position amphibolically indicates a homosexual encounter as Frédéric Serralta has indicated (83 note 9). This underlying meaning behind this metaphorical swordplay was surely quite obvious to the knowing spectator:

> JUAN RANA: Esto es mucho peor por Jesu Christo
> PÉREZ: Vida del alma, que tu amor celebra.
> JUAN RANA: Acabose, por Dios que me requiebra. (226)

> JUAN RANA: This is much worse, by God
> PÉREZ: Light of my life, this celebrates your love.
> JUAN RANA: I'm doomed, he's starting to sweet-talk me.

Juan Rana now seems to understand the full meaning of the amorous threat by Juan Pérez and fears it more than the earlier physical one. On another level, Juan Pérez alludes to Juan Rana's well-known type of love. Possibly, Juan Rana wishes Juan Pérez to stop because he is afraid of literally falling to pieces, as the verb *requebrar* would indicate, which, while metaphorically signifying sweet-talk, literally means to rebreak an already fragile item. There is, therefore, an undeniably sexual double meaning in this line. Alzieu et al. list numerous erotic poems in the vocabulary section where *acabar* means to reach orgasm for both men and women (329). *Quebrar* might imply the result of Juan Pérez's forceful pelvic thrusts. Cela also has shown *quebrar* to be a euphemism for castration or emasculation (289). As a result, this verbal simulation of an act of buggery not only indicates the violence of the sexual act on the part of Juan Pérez but also implies Juan Rana's lack of masculinity.

From physical and metaphorical frolicking, the fencers would seem to move on to a duel of semantic opposites.

> PÉREZ: Mi Angel.
> JUAN RANA: Mi Demonio.
> PÉREZ: Mi fiel verdad.
> JUAN RANA: Mi falso testimonio.
> PÉREZ: Mi amor es bueno.
> JUAN RANA: Pues parece malo. (226–7)

PÉREZ:	My angel.
JUAN RANA:	My demon.
PÉREZ:	My honest truth.
JUAN RANA:	My false witness.
PÉREZ:	My love is good.
JUAN RANA:	Well it seems bad.

While Juan Pérez considers Juan Rana his angel, the latter sees his cohort as a devil. If for Juan Pérez Juan Rana is a true sign of his love, the latter sees him as a false representation or testimony of love; Juan Rana may even be implying that his arrest was due to 'false testimony' by witnesses, a common occurrence for many accused of the *pecado nefando*. Indeed, if Juan Pérez speaks of the goodness of his love, Juan Rana sees it from an opposite point of view. This is very much a tongue-in-cheek repartee considering that it is the recently arrested Juan Rana who is aghast at and taken aback by the libidinous proposals of Juan Pérez.

The dialogue at this point returns to the realm of the phallic:

PÉREZ:	Hazme favor de darme.
JUAN RANA:	Con un palo.
PÉREZ:	Has de darme la mano.
JUAN RANA:	Si la quiere de açotes, tome hermano.
	De amistades perfectas.
	Valgate Barrabas, y lo que aprietas. (227)

PÉREZ:	Please give it to me.
JUAN RANA:	With a stick.
PÉREZ:	You have to give me your hand on it.
JUAN RANA:	I will if you want a beating, take it, brother.
	I give it willingly.
	Holy, Barrabas! How you squeeze!

If we consider the implications of the verb *dar* and *palo* that we have seen in the analysis of *El desafío de Juan Rana*, we see there is a clear indication of a homosexual meaning here. Juan Rana replies to Juan Pérez's wish to take his hand – a double meaning that infers a marriage union – with a violent threat of a thrashing or *mano de azotes* (*Diccionario de Autoridades*). He qualifies his threat with the expression *de amistades perfectas*. Javier Pérez Escohotado explains that the euphemism *relación perfecta* was used in the legal and religious jargon of the day to identify sexual relations between people of the same sex (174). It would seem, therefore, that Juan Rana refers to a 'perfect,' homosexual relationship. When contact actually occurs, Juan Rana remarks on the force Juan Pérez is exerting while cleverly leaving unclear what Juan Pérez is actually squeezing. However, the expression *apretar la mano*, to squeeze hands, is a signal of mutual intentions between lovers. In this sense Juan Pérez, in the forceful squeezing of one of Juan Rana's appendages – be it the hand or something else – is giving a sexual signal. On another level, however, when used in the context of punishment, this same phrase means to punish with a heavier hand. This second meaning ties in with the implied violence of this encounter and the underlying fear by the homosexual of being caught and brutally tortured or killed for this crime against nature. Considering the audience's complicit knowledge of Juan Rana's recent arrest, the implicit double meanings of the text up to this point must surely have been quite effective in inferring the humourous homosexual meaning to its receptors.

Quickly, however, there is a change in the sexual implications that have appeared up to this point in the dialogue:

PÉREZ: Dandome por mujer tu hermana hermosa.
JUAN RANA: Esso es?
PÉREZ: Claro está.
JUAN RANA: No es otra cosa?
PÉREZ: Que aviades pensado?
JUAN RANA: Lo que vos si os huvieran requebrado. (227)

PÉREZ: We're shaking on your giving me your sister for a wife.
JUAN RANA: That's what we're doing?
PÉREZ: Obviously.
JUAN RANA: Not something else?
PÉREZ: What were you thinking?
JUAN RANA: What you would have thought if you had been sweet-talked.

Obviously the spectator, like Juan Rana, has been strung along in believing another meaning, as Arellano et al. also note (656 note 33). In this way, the audience, like Juan Rana, has been misinterpreting Juan Pérez's words. The audience is ultimately manipulated and, indeed, tricked, like the onstage Juan Rana. The spectators must surely have revelled in their amphibolic understanding of the double 'other' jocose meaning and, then, the sudden semantic and sexual about-face.

This dialogue plays on a common occurrence of clandestine homosexual activity – the misinterpretation of ambiguous and indirect sexual signals. The farcical misinterpretation of gay signs combined with Juan Rana's offstage life is obviously the basis of the humour here. This use of homosexuality is by no means moralistically condemning. On the contrary, the playful use of Juan Rana's documented 'irregular' sexuality shows that Quiñones de Benavente makes the most of the actor's sexuality, using it as the main vehicle for humour in this dialogue.

El mundo al revés was also written by Quiñones de Benavente and first published in the collection *Entremeses nuevos* published in Zaragoza in 1643 (Bergman 355). Curiously, two other variants of this work exist under the titles *El soldado* and *El mundo*. Bergman explains that *El soldado*, while published in *Joco Seria*, the most authoritative collection of Quiñones de Benavente's works, remains notably incomplete (355). She also notes that *El mundo* is an 'incorrect' copy of *El soldado*. She adds that *El mundo al revés*, while shorter than the other two, adds thirty-two verses at the end that are missing in the other versions, as well as a 16-verse dance that was not in *El soldado*. These additions are of great significance for the true gay meaning of the text. It can be speculated that the absence of these verses is, perhaps, an indication of censorship or, at least, self-censorship on the part of Quiñones de Benavente. These revealing additions to *El mundo al revés* make this version the one of choice for our analysis.[8] While the metaphorical sword and swordplay are absent from *El mundo al revés*, the soldier as metaphor is significant to this *entremés* and central to the analysis.

This *entremés* would seem to be about Juan Rana forgetting what profession he has and, indeed, who he is:

Yo soy un hombre, señores,
porque no puedo ser dos;
yo soy, en efecto un hombre,
¡válgame Dios! ¿Quién soy?
Por Dios que se me ha olvidado:
perdonademe aqueste error,
que no soy de los primeros
que se olvidan de quien son.
¡Alto!, yo voy á sabello

de mundo en el obrador,
que apenas entraré cuando
mis obras digan quién son. (747)

I am a man, gentlemen,
for I cannot be two;
I am, in effect, a man.
God help me! Who am I?
By God who has forsaken me,
forgive me this error,
for I am not one of the first
who have forgotten who they are.
Stop! I'm going to find out
when I act,
because as soon as I get on stage
my acts will tell me who I am.

It is, of course, to be taken tongue-in-cheek that the most famous *gracioso* of this time and a major drawing card for the public should suffer from stage amnesia. That his character should immediately see the need to emphasize that he is indeed a man hints not only at his short, unmanly stature but also at his well-known arrest. His parodic malady and an ensuing encounter with el Mundo – a female character playing the part of the all-knowing World – serves as a vehicle for questioning the true profession and identity of the confused Juan Rana.

El Mundo asks Juan Rana if he is a messenger, tavern owner, or barber but he rejects all of these professions for their typical negative reputation. However, Juan Rana is finally recognized by a fellow countryman who calls him 'Señor alférez mayor' (747), the standard- or flag-bearer of a company of soldiers. After a string of questions, this time concerning his battle experiences, the exasperated Juan Rana asks: '¿Hay mundo con más preguntas?/¿Es mundo ó interrogatorio?' (747) (Is there a world with more questions? / Is this a world or an interrogation room?). Significantly, the now flustered Juan Rana typically and significantly misinterprets what has earlier been said: 'Estos señores decían que era alfiler mayor' (747) (These gentlemen said that I was a big pink). Literally, *alfiler* is a pin, and while this hyperbole would certainly be a comic description of Juan Rana as a *gracioso* who pointedly pricks the other actors into action, there is another meaning behind this misinterpretation, or more precisely its pejorative slang equivalent, fag. As the analysis of *El desafío de Juan Rana* has shown, *alfiler* is a metaphor for homosexual. Juan Rana's persona, in misunderstanding his given profession, has, therefore, amphibolically hinted at his homosexuality (see note 4). In *El soldado* there is a different variant to Juan Rana's encounter with his fellow countryman:

SALVADOR: Señor alférez mayor,
                    ¿Hay tal dicha?
JUAN RANA: ¿Quién es alfiler mayor aquí?
SALVADOR: Usted.
JUAN RANA: Es mentira (Cotarelo y Mori 585).

SALVADOR: Sir Bearer of the Flag,
                    Is there such a destiny?
JUAN RANA: Who is a big fag?
SALVADOR: You.
JUAN RANA: That's a lie.

In this version Juan Rana's 'professional' misunderstanding immediately follows Salvador's statement. When Salvador does not correct the semantic error on the part of Juan Rana and answers affirmatively 'usted,' he is in fact labelling Juan Rana a homosexual. When Juan Rana calls the affirmation a lie, he is ironically negating a fact that is well known to the audience, considering that he had been recently arrested for the *pecado nefando*. Indeed, his frustration at being questioned in such detail would seem to refer to his recent interrogation after being arrested for the *pecado nefando*.

An important part of the thirty-two additional verses of *El mundo al revés* reaffirm the hypothesis that Juan Rana's onstage interrogation refers to his offstage recent arrest:

Señor Mundo, yo confieso
que como de un año acá
han hecho tantos potajes
de mi persona venial,
se me olvidó de quién era.   (747)

O World, I confess
that a year ago
they made such a mishmash
of my venial person,
that I forgot who I was.

It would seem that the Juan Rana persona is referring here to the terrible experience he endured under questioning in the not-so-distant past. In this context, it is understandable that the mishmash made of his person by the authorities should have made him forget who he actually was. The choice of the adjective 'venial' is important considering that it refers to a misdemeanour, easily forgiven. In other words, Juan Rana would seem to be complaining that his arrest and subsequent interrogation were 'much ado about nothing' considering the levity of his onstage and offstage 'crimes.'

With the other actors now explaining that in the recent past Juan Rana has played a bullfighter, a mayor, a poet, and finally a lawyer – all types of his well-known repertoire – the actor would seem to be gaining strength in his explanation for his staged amnesia:

> Pues desa suerte, señores,
> disculpado puedo estar,
> pues si yo no me conozco
> muchos en el mundo habrá
> que no sepan lo que son
> por verse en alto lugar. (747)

> Well in this way, gentlemen,
> I can be forgiven;
> if I don't know myself,
> there are many people in the world
> who don't know who they are
> for being in high places.

This passage is also an obvious criticism of the hypocrisy of those who have moved on to 'higher places,' forgetting in their ascent who they really are. As the *entremés* concludes, the other actors feel the need to censure Juan Rana's harsh comments against those in positions of authority:

> MUJER I: Calle, que éste es entremés
> Y se pasa á murmurar.
> JUAN RANA: Luego decir la verdad
> ¿se llama pecado ya?
> SALVADOR: Sí, porque agora en el mundo
> no se sabe dónde ésta.

JUAN RANA: Allá diz que ésta en el cielo;
               chitón, callar, callar,
               porque aqueste es entremés.   (747–8)

WOMAN 1:   Be quiet; this is an *entremés*
            and later people will gossip.
JUAN RANA: To tell the truth,
            Is that now a sin?
SALVADOR: Yes, because in today's world
            we don't know where it is.
JUAN RANA: They say it's in heaven;
            Quiet, hush up, hush up,
            for this is an *entremés*.

In this way, the others on stage act as if they are afraid of being over-heard speaking against authority and play at self-censorship. The 'criminal' Juan Rana, on the other hand, with friends in high places, would seem to be testing the limits of political satire. Juan Rana's mask does finally succumb to peer pressure but only after pretending to be surprised that telling the truth should be considered a crime. In his final words Juan Rana states that truth is up in the air. This would seem to refer to the fact that life and the rules that regulate it are precarious or, in other words, very much in the air. Indeed the world in which he lived would seem to be *un mundo al revés*.

Quiñones de Benavente's *El mundo al revés* mocks the repressive and hypocritical nature of society where speaking the truth is considered sinful. As the carnivalesque title suggests, such hypocrisy represents a world gone topsy-turvy. This most certainly refers to Juan Rana and others like him who are forced to lead a double life in a 'qué dirán' society preoccupied with appearances and honour rather than the truth. Indeed, Juan Rana's irregular sexuality is a sinful truth that must not be discussed openly, although it can be used amphibolically to parody society as a whole.

In Francisco Bernardo de Quirós's *Las fiestas del aldea* the sword once again appears and as in *El mundo al revés*, Juan Rana's real life experiences can be seen to be the basis for important scenes.[9] Decidedly, implicit gay double entendres show that the audience would have to be in on the *pecado nefando* joke of the text and, indeed, know the lurid details of Juan Rana's arrest. The arrest and its details are the unguarded main vehicle for humour – without them, little if any humour can be found in the text. The playwright was appointed for life as an *aguacil* of the royal court and like many other members of the court he was a prize-winning writer (La Barrera y Leirado 314). Of particular interest is the fact that his *Obras ... y Aventuras de don Fruela* (1656) was prohibited by the Inquisition. This collection included a novel, a burlesque comedy, and ten *entremeses* (314). *Las fiestas del aldea* was one of the ten *entremeses* included in this banned book. Javier Huerta Calvo explains that these *entremeses* were inserted within the narrative of the novel as a means of distraction for the reader (*Teatro Breve de los siglos XVI y XVII* 236). While Huerta Calvo's introductory note to *Las fiestas del aldea* concludes that the works were not favourably looked upon by the Inquisitional censors due to the religious parody of the *autos sacramentales,* we can conjecture as well that the sexual parody was also deemed objectionable. In this way, while bellicose imagery is once again used, the precise details of Juan Rana's *pecado nefando* past make this *entremés* more personal and 'incriminating' in nature.

Las fiestas del aldea begins with the Hidalgo character reproaching Juan Rana for the vice of gluttony, a great dishonour for a fellow mayor:

> ¿No es deshonor de tan honrado oficio
> que digan que un Alcalde tiene vicio
> de comer cuanto traen postura
> que no le hiciera una cabalgadura? (237)

> Isn't it dishonouring this noble office
> that they say that a mayor has the vice
> of eating more food than
> a packhorse can bring him?

While the sin of gluttony was a notable trait of the Juan Rana mask, it was also a typical subject during the celebrations surrounding Easter, the period when *autos* and many *entremeses* were performed. It cannot be forgotten, as well, that hunger was not an unknown condition or literary theme during the baroque period. The Hidalgo recites a list of products on which Juan Rana has overindulged that include cheese, meat, and finally, the neighbour's nephew's wine. To each of the Hidalgo's questions, Juan Rana has a comical rebuttal to explain his *gourmandise.* This conversation is, however, a prelude to the rest of the *entremés,* which consists of the actors watching a mock and mocking production of a Lope de Vega *auto sacramental* entitled *Del amor y la gallina ciega.* During

this parodic production of the *auto* Juan Rana acts the part of a boisterous, interrupting, and simple audience member. The *entremés* is not only
a mockery of Lope's *auto* but also of the theatre audience.

Of interest to this study is the comical and revealing rebuttal of Juan
Rana to his friend's question concerning the neighbour's nephew's
wine:

HIDALGO: ¿Por qué anoche al sobrino del vecino
              le bebistes el vino?
JUAN RANA: Dije: '¿Quién va a la ronda, camarada?'
              Y respondióme un hombre con su espada,
              y mirándola yo con gran chacota,
              la espada me enseñó, y era una bota;
              el vino que tenía me bebí,
              y la bota sin vino le volví,
              y dije: 'Pues que ya la que da es dada,
              la vaina os vuelvo, y llevadme la espada.' (238)

HIDALGO: Why did you drink the neighbour's
              nephew's wine last night?
JUAN RANA: I said to him, 'Who goes there, friend?'
              And a man answered me with his sword,
              and seeing it, I got very excited;
              he showed me his sword, and it was a wineskin;
              I drank its wine,
              and I returned the wineskin empty,
              and said: 'Now that that which gives is given,
              I return the sheath; now bear my sword.'

On a straight level, Juan Rana would seem to have met an unknown
character in the dark and called out for him to identify himself. This
mysterious gentleman answered him with what appears to be his uplifted
sword that turns out to be a wineskin, which he gives to Juan Rana, who
drains it. This interpretation is, of course, lacking in logic, interest, and
humour as Serralta has noted: 'Soso y pesado nos parece el cuenticillo, a
no ser que se recurra al sentido erótico de "dar," "vaina," y "espada"
acompañado por el actor con una posible puntuación gestual' (89) (The
anecdote seems bland and boring, unless it is referring to the erotic
sense of *dar*, *vaina*, and *espada*, accompanied by possible punctuating
gestures by the actor). While Serralta recognizes the homosexual double

meaning of the text, he, nonetheless, concludes that it would be tedious and repetitive to continue commenting on this and other examples of this type which occur in the text (89). But, without this second meaning and the analysis of it, there would be no humour at all in the passage, as Serralta admits. Though he does not wish to pursue this interpretation, Serralta does, nonetheless, cite the lexical glossary of Alzieu et al. for those who wish to do so.

On an initial level, Juan Rana's use of 'camarada' could have a homosexual overtone. *Camarada* refers to a roommate or bedfellow. As we have seen, *espada* is a phallic symbol and *dar* is a euphemism for fornication. *Vaina*, on the other hand, refers to the scrotum (Cela 2:119, 120–1, 224). In the context of this *entremés*, however, 'bota' would seem to refer both to the scrotum/sperm container and to the large and enlarged penis of the neighbour's nephew. Therefore, this passage describes the genitals shown to Juan Rana by the neighbour's nephew upon which Juan Rana looks with glee. The 'bota' (scrotum) returned empty would appear to refer to a completed act of fellatio performed by Juan Rana. David F. Greenberg observes that 'many of the male homosexual relations of the time were pederastic ... Some of these relationships endured, but many must have ended when the youthful partner reached adulthood' (309–10). It should also be remembered that Juan Rana's real-life 'partner in crime' was a youthful page just as here his 'dramatic' partner is the young nephew of his neighbour. Juan Rana, therefore, returns the *bota* as an emptied *vaina* – perhaps he is offering his own 'sword' now that he has consumed that which was given. We are not yet privy, however, to whether this reciprocal act was carried out.

The scribe, who is also a party to this conversation, pipes up, complaining about an encounter with the same young man:

> También, anoche en unas cuchilladas
> me dejó y se apartó dando risadas,
> diciendo el mal cristiano:
> 'Yo no recibo, denle al Escribano.' (238)

> Also, last night in a brawl
> he abandoned me and ran off laughing,
> saying, the heathen:
> 'I don't receive, give it to the scribe.'

On the surface, the young man would appear to be refusing to take blows from his opponents in a brawl, suggesting that they instead hit the scribe. On another level, the young man's revealing words indicate that he does not 'receive' and suggest that the scribe does. Clearly, the youth is not a passive sexual partner but rather an active one. Indeed, the laughing nephew represents the person in control, the person in a sexual position of power. Juan Rana would seem to misunderstand the line 'denle al Escribano' and the scribe's discontent at being given something. Indeed, Juan Rana expresses his belief that one was always supposed to make the scribe happy by giving him things. As an example, whenever he is offered 'refrescos' (refreshments) or other things, he replies, 'no puedo recibirlos ... hermano/ que so Alcalde, contente al Escribano' (238) (I cannot receive them, ... brother/ for I am the mayor, please the scribe). While the meaning of *contentar* in this passage is clearly to please, and although the manner of giving pleasure is not specified, Alzieu et al. does provide two poetic examples where this verb refers to sexual fulfilment through penetration (37, poem 25, l. 2; 246, poem 126, l. 8). In this context, therefore, *refresco* could be considered a euphemism for the penis and its revitalizing properties. Of course *refresco* refers to a refreshment, such as a drink, and could ultimately, therefore, be considered a euphemism for semen. In suggesting that such *refrescos* be given to the scribe, Juan Rana again reinforces the idea that the scribe receives in the sexual sense.

As such, this *entremés* contains a highly charged depiction of clandestine sexual encounters between men. In many ways, the analysed passages show that the *entremés* as a whole is testing the limits of acceptable societal and sexual parody. The extent of this testing is only evident with a complete analysis of the gay meaning. On another level, the bawdy portrayal of a sexual encounter between Juan Rana and a younger man surely refers to the actor's personal experience. In this case, the age difference between the two 'fencers' reflects Juan Rana's arresting encounter with a young page. In other words, the level of amphibology is quite clear because of the well-known past of Juan Rana. Considering the gay humour in Bernardo de Quirós's *Las fiestas del aldea*, it is not surprising that the Inquisition censors should find his *Obras* 'offensive.' Undoubtedly, however, the audience revelled in its irreverence.

Perhaps the most incriminating Juan Rana *entremés* of this analysis – on the level of a gay meaning – is Quiñones de Benavente's *El pipote en nombre de Juan Rana*.[10] Bergman states that the play was written when Juan Rana was already at the height of his fame (432). This statement is valid considering that in the beginning Salvador, another actor in the play,[11] gives 'una larga alabanza del talento de Cosme en las tablas' (432) (a long speech in praise of Cosme's onstage talents). This lauding preamble is followed by the *burla*, which makes up the main body of the text. Here Juan Rana helps Salvador to win a woman from the grip of her overbearing and jealous brother Pipote by playing the part of an obnoxious and obtrusive deaf man. As in the case of *Las fiestas del aldea* it is the introductory dialogue, however, that is of interest to us. Indeed, while these opening passages are certainly laudatory, they are also quite revealing, as Bergman recognizes: 'Lo que sigue, la equivocación de Juan Rana creyéndose requebrado con intención pecaminosa, podría interpretarse como alusión al prendimiento de Pérez en otoño de 1636' (432) (What follows, Juan Rana's error in believing that he has been flattered with sinful intentions, could be interpreted as an allusion to Pérez's arrest in the fall of 1636). As we have shown, Juan Rana's arrest and the *pecado nefando* theme are as one, an integral part of his person and persona. Indeed, Salvador in the same breath speaks of Juan Rana the transvestite actor and the person arrested for the nefarious sin. In contrast to the *entremeses* analysed earlier in this chapter, no metaphorical bellicose camouflaging of Juan Rana's on- and offstage irregular sexuality is in evidence.

In the first lines of this *entremés*, as Bergman has indicated, Salvador speaks of Juan Rana's successes and popularity with audiences:

Pues, para todo ensillado
Cosme a quien confirmo la turba humana
explendido banquete a donde sirves
platos a barias gentes
todos de rana y todos diferentes
cosquillas generales
que las hazen en todos los corrales. (714)

Cosme, you are eveready,
as the crowd shows;
it's a splendid banquet where you serve up
dishes to varied people,
all by Rana and all different;
you make people laugh
as they do in all theatres.

This metaphorical banquet where the many and varied *Rana* dishes are of mass appeal accurately sums up Juan Rana's successful acting career. Juan Rana's reply, however, indicates that Salvador's banquet homage must be taken 'with a grain of salt': 'con el hablar y el gesto/ dios de mi alma en que a de parar esto' (714) (with voice and gesture/ Good Lord, where is it going to stop?). Juan Rana seems to be exasperated and does not know when the flattery will stop.

Immediately following Juan Rana's concerned remarks, Salvador elaborates on his description of the Juan Rana career and mask:

> Simple discreto que por tu donayre
> mereciste que fueses perpetuo
> alcalde de los entremeses
> dando al bulgo sentencias avisadas (714)

> Humble, just, for your wittiness
> you earned the right to be perpetual
> mayor of *entremeses,*
> giving the public wise words

Salvador outlines that Juan Rana's acting qualities merit that he be known as the famous interpreter of the infamous bumbling mayor role. At the end of his more detailed description of Juan Rana's acting ability and career, Salvador allows Juan Rana to speak. Juan Rana's own explanation represents the meat of our *pecado nefando* analysis of this *entremés.*

The ensuing long passage can be considered a confessional by Juan Rana not only of his irregular acting but also of his other life. This other interpretation, while bold in its initial stages, comes together in the final lines of the passage in a crescendo-like fashion. Juan Rana begins his declaration, saying:

> mi señor es aqueste requebrarme
> porque por dios que aunque es caso terrible
> que me temo segun soy de apacible
> quando aya usado sartas de mujeres
> sal por aquesta calle
> y toparas un talle y otro talle
> mas tiesos que un virote
> que sin hazer por que les dan garrote
> dexandolos tan largos y delgados (714)

> My sir, is that flattery?
> Because by God although it is a terrible thing
> I'm afraid, I'm such a weak man
> that I have used women's baubles.

> Go out into the street
> and you'll bump into one figure and another
> more constricted than shackles,
> for no reason being squeezed so hard
> that they're left so long and thin

Juan Rana asks if Salvador is trying to flatter him. Then, quite literally, Juan Rana states that he has worn women's adornments – Sebastián de Covarrubias Otozco defines *sarta* as a necklace for women made of different pieces strung together and more precisely, he states that it can be a string of pearls or gold or silver pieces. But figuratively, Juan Rana could also mean that he has performed a string of female roles one after the other. At first it might seem that Juan Rana's self-defence would be a critique of women's fashion in general. He speaks of the *talle* or waist of people on the street, so tightly drawn as to be torturously reshaped into a long and thin form. Importantly, however, the gender of the people is not noted; and Juan Rana has often worn women's clothing as an actor. Therefore, if homoerotically symbolic meanings of *talle* (size of the penis [Alzieu et al. 189, poem 97, note to l. 5 of poem]), and *virote* (penis [225 l. 35 of poem in note 14]) are considered, these passages can unblushingly refer to the conspicuous state of an erect penis visible under transvestite clothing. It must be remembered that *garrote* also refers to a wooden rod that can be held in the hand, and is used in the expression *tieso como un garrote*, or, firm as a rod (Covarrubias 581). Ironically, as well, the illicit flaunting of the erect sex organ contrasts with the title's 'pipote,' a small tube used to contain and transport liquids and other things, which here refers to Juan Rana's member. Marjorie Garber's reference to Dr Robert Stoller's medical observations on the male-to-female transvestite's gender trouble are pertinent here:

> The transvestite fights a battle against being destroyed by feminine desires, first by alternating his masculinity with female behavior, and thus reassuring himself that it isn't permanent; and second, by being always aware even at the height of feminine behavior – when he is fully dressed in woman's clothes – that he has the absolute insignia of maleness, a penis. And there is no more acute awareness of its presence that when he is assuringly experiencing it with an erection. (95)

This interpretation, while seemingly hypothetical, at this point is, however, thematically linked to the actor's allusion to onstage cross-dressing.

Juan Rana continues with what can be considered a description of the girdled female body:

... ay muger que trae no sin mancilla
enbasada la carne de la costilla
tan estrecha y gazisa [?]
que ya no es talle sino longaniza (714)

... there are women who, not without moving us to pity,
wear the meat on their ribs packed
so tightly and stretched [?]
that they no longer have a figure, but a link of sausage

Juan Rana speaks of 'women' who carry the meat stored on their ribs in such restrictive manner that it moves one to grief. He explains that this tight packing technique makes the meat so elongated that it resembles a link of sausage. On a different level, there would seem to be a phallic and transvestite interpretation of this text. In this analytical vein, 'mujer' would refer, therefore, to the professional male prostitute/transvestite who dresses as a woman to attract male customers. This professional dressing up is quite obviously in opposition to Juan Rana's theatrical transvestism.

This daring gay and transvestite reading which could still seem tentative at this point holds more weight with Juan Rana's revealing final lines:

busca estas savandijas
y a mi dexame yr y no me aflixas
que ay puerta de alcala por dios eterno
y para mí traer aun el ynbierno
quando el frio haze fieros
mas apetezco fuentes que braseros. (714)

go after those low-lifes
and let me go, and don't persecute me.
There is a Puerta de Alcalá, after all!
Rather, for me bring on even the winter.
When the cold is fierce,
I prefer fountains to braziers.

Marybeth Hamilton's assertion that onstage cross-dressing often went hand in hand with offstage prostitution would explain, perhaps, Juan Rana's attempt to dissociate himself from these *sabandijas* or 'low-lifes' (116). His onstage wish not to be bothered by or associated with these 'other' transvestites would seem to allude to the bad memories of his real life arrest and questioning at the Puerta de Alcalá tribunals. The Puerta de Alcalá was, of course, the location where homosexuals were taken for questioning upon their arrest. Notwithstanding his tongue-in-cheek dissociation from his 'sister' transvestites, Juan Rana ends his repartee in an extremely revealing manner: 'quando el frio haze fieros/ mas apetezco fuentes que braseros' (714). On one level, Juan Rana fears man's cold nature that gives him the brutish capability to burn another at the stake like a 'faggot.' To be burnt at the stake was, of course, a common punishment for those 'guilty' of the *pecado nefando*. In this sense, Juan Rana opts for the wet element of nature rather than the 'all consuming' element of fire. *Fuente* as in 'tray' is also semantically linked to the earlier mentioned 'platos' and the banquet metaphor in general that described the varied career and performance of Juan Rana. Continuing with the homoerotic interpretation of the text, however, *fuente* is a source for water and more specifically, a hose. *Agua* is, of course, a euphemism for semen (Alzieu et al. 98, poem 62, l. 1).[12] Indeed, *fuente* can also be seen to refer to testicles because testicles produce semen as a hose produces water (Cela 1:199). Juan Rana would unabashedly seem to be saying, therefore, that sexually he prefers *fuentes* or the penis to *braseros* or *cunnus* (Alzieu et al. 60, poem 42, l. 8). Significantly, this would represent an 'open' confession of sexual preference by the Juan Rana person/persona.

The dialogue that follows between Juan Rana and Salvador supports the gay meaning of the text:

SALVADOR:	estoy difunto
	estoy ennamorado que me quemo
JUAN RANA:	oygan pues eso es lo que yo me quemo[13]
SALVADOR:	estoy ennamorado
	mi señor de la hermana de un letrado
	mas bizarra y lozana que el sol
JUAN RANA:	hablara yo para mañana
	que amor de hembra a sido
	valgate barravas qual me as tenido (714)

SALVADOR: I'm finished
            I'm in love, I'm burning up.
JUAN RANA: Hey! That's what's burning me up.
SALVADOR: I'm in love,
            sir, with the sister of a learned man,
            more bright and beautiful than the sun.
JUAN RANA: This is all for nothing
            as he was talking about the love of a woman.
            Holy, Barrabas! You had me going.

What we have in this passage is a misinterpretation of sexual innuendoes strikingly similar to the encounter between Juan Pérez and Juan Rana in *Los muertos vivos*, as Bergman has noted (522). As in *Los muertos vivos* Juan Rana is surprised (and possibly relieved or dissapointed) on learning that Salvador's burning love is not directed at him but rather at a woman.

Ultimately, the homoerotic *El pipote en nombre de Juan Rana* constitutes an amphibolic affirmation of gayness on the part of the Juan Rana stage persona, histrionically and historically linked to his offstage person. Considering that *El pipote en nombre de Juan Rana* was produced between 1636 and 1640 – dates that coincide with Juan Rana's arrest – it is clear that the humour of the preliminary dialogue between Juan Rana and his 'straight' man alludes to the *pecado nefando*. This is a defiant mockery of the era's official sexual mores and represents a self-outing on the part of Juan Rana.

The *pecado nefando entremeses* created an inverted reality where the norms of society were parodied. Specifically written and produced for an audience predisposed to topical and amphibolic humour, they provided a place where the marginal and the immoral took main-stage for a short and controlled period of time. It is '[n]o wonder the Spanish moralists felt their power was threatened by the perceived physical and moral excesses or freedoms of the *corral* and theatricalized social events' (Connor 424). Although it is difficult and on occasion 'risky/risqué' to assign gay meanings to texts produced for immediate and pleasurable consumption by a seventeenth-century audience, the analysis of the Juan Rana persona has proven fruitful. Evidently Spanish baroque theatre relished homo-sexual/erotic double entendres as the *entremeses* of this analysis show.

Notwithstanding, the use of homosexual references here must be seen for what it truly is – laughter at the expense of the 'other.' The homosexual, one of the most hated and persecuted minorities in history, is considered fair game for mockery. He is presented stereotypically as a gullible, henpecked, weak, cowardly, cuckolded, and ultimately laughable man. He is used, therefore, as a scapegoat or *pharmakos* for the ills of society. On the other side of the coin, while he presents a negative image of homosexuality, its theatrical and comic depiction nonetheless is a testimony to its prevalence and power to fuel the imagination. Perhaps in the end the best medicine against repression and hatred is to face the oppressor on his or her terms as Juan Rana did throughout his successful and long theatrical career as a *gracioso*.

While *El desafío de Juan Rana* uses the phallus/sword to parody homosexual behaviour and criticize the empire, other swordplays are less condemning. In Francisco Bernardo de Quirós's *Las fiestas del aldea* the sword once again appears but as in *El mundo al revés*, more precise details of Juan Rana's personal life are given.[14] In this way, while bellicose imagery is once again used, the precise details of his *pecado nefando* in the past make this *entremés* more 'incriminating' and personal in nature. As in *El mundo al revés*, Juan Rana's real life experiences are the basis for important scenes. Decidedly, implicit gay double entendres show that the audience would have to be in on the *pecado nefando* joke of the text and, indeed, know the lurid details of Juan Rana's arrest. The arrest and its details are the unguarded main vehicle for humour – without them, little humour if any can be found in the text. Indeed, Quiñones de Benavente's foregrounding of Juan Rana's arrest and his constant rewriting of it as a comic event serves to subvert the laws against sodomy, albeit temporally, onstage. Ultimately, we must marvel at the astonishing boldness of these authors and actors (especially Juan Rana) and ardently applaud their spirited subversiveness, as did the baroque audience.

5 The Triumphant Juan Rana

Juan Rana enjoyed a long and highly successful career within one of the most important theatrical traditions and periods in all of Europe, the Spanish Golden Age. Significantly, the playwrights who wrote for him and the public who cheered him on invented a mask that could rival those of the commedia dell'arte tradition and this during his own lifetime. Remarkably, as this study of Juan Rana's person/persona has demonstrated, much of Juan Rana's favoured and famed stature and the essence of his invented mask was a product of an ambiguous and amphibolic portrayal of homosexuality.

The 'self-reflective' Juan Rana created an ambiguous identity within a staged world that caused a metaphysical questioning of identity and reality on the part of the spectator. The end result was a thought-provoking creation of an illusory space somewhere between illusion and reality. Juan Rana's in-between identity 'crisis' directly correlates with his sexuality, ambiguously unfixed between the socially constructed extremes of the male and female. This seemingly indefinable sexuality is outrageously evident in the many transvestite roles played by Juan Rana. This cross-dressed mockery of gender differentiation and the analogous engendered labour codes challenged the preconceived constructs of phallocentric power and biological difference. While the need to read in between the lines was shown to co-exist with visible manifestations of difference, amphibolic understanding became central in the bellicose *entremeses*. The gay significance of the fencer and his playful use of phallic paraphernalia is pivotal to understanding the homosexual puns and wordplay of the text. What perhaps would appear to be an insistence on the 'in-betweenness' of the Juan Rana person/persona, ultimately holds a weighty significance.

Etymologically, *entremés* denotes in-betweenness; the one-act play comes between the acts of the main play. Coming between the acts of the main play, it effectively interrupts its longer counterpart in more ways than one. While the *entremés* physically and temporally suspends the other production, the bawdy and raucous acting and themes of the *entremés* can also be seen to disrupt the ambience and flow created by its 'better theatrical half.' This potential for disruption does not end within the confines of the theatre and its production. While the subversive, risky and risqué subject matter that characterizes the *entremés* can be seen as playful, it, nonetheless, represents an insubordinate and, hence, inherently disruptive attack on traditional values. The religious and political censorship of many *entremeses* during the baroque period is proof that the potential for defiance and sacrilege was well understood by the authorities of the day. In this way, the *entremés*, while seemingly an innocuous and high-spirited means to appease and entertain, can be considered a danger to lawful societal gender roles and sexual mores. Therefore, the *entremés* in its essence represents an in-between state incorporating both the lawful and the lawless.

Historically, the baroque period can also be considered to represent a period of in-betweenness. The many divisive shifts in the political, military, and economic status of Spain during this period created a society where instability and drastic change were the norm. Beginning in the latter part of the sixteenth-century, with the dissolution of the Charles V's great empire, Spain suffered a steady decline in political, military, and economic power. Exemplifying this divided decline is Phillip II's reign marred by revolt and defeat. The further loss of Spanish imperial power suffered during his rule is best characterized by the famous defeat of the 'invincible' Spanish Armada at the hands of the English. In his obsessive attempt to maintain Spain's Catholicism intact, Phillip II closed the country's borders to the outside world. This entrapment fostered a long-reaching pessimism among Spanish intellectuals.

On the death of Phillip II in 1598, his weak and inexperienced son Phillip III acceded the throne and as Melveena McKendrick has pointed out,

> [t]his period of unsurpassed literary brilliance and splendour at court was also the age when the cancer of Spain's growing ills rose to the surface and proceeded to devour the visible as well as the hidden body of Spain. (4)

Phillip III (1598–1621) and his son who followed him, Phillip IV (1621–65), were incapable of governing and handed the reins of power over to their right-hand men. The court that once imposed austerity under the rule of Phillip II now enjoyed an ambiance of frivolity and extravagance known, or, perhaps more accurately, infamous throughout the rest of Europe, which generally disapproved. This lavish decadence, which culminated in the reign of Phillip IV, was in great contrast to 'ravages of war, famine, pestilence and poverty' (McKendrick 4) that existed outside the palace walls. Even if the reign of the last Hapsburg, the mentally and physically deficient Charles II (1665–1700), saw some economic reprieve, it was, nonetheless, marred by corruption and warfare.

Considering that Juan Rana was born sometime during the latter part of the sixteenth century and died in 1672, his life and career spanned much of this tumultuous period of historical and societal in-betweenness. Physically a short and roly-poly caricature of a man and sexually an 'aberration,' Juan Rana astonishingly profited by what could be considered his imperfections. It would seem that against all odds – including the many theatre closings for royal mourning – Juan Rana survived to live a long and successful life. As the undisputed star of the baroque *entremés* with his multiple manifestations of his ambiguous and amphibolic modus operandi, Juan Rana could rightfully be dubbed the Spanish Golden Age's 'Mr In-Between.' In many ways, Juan Rana, like the *entremés* itself, can be seen to emblematically represent Spain, a society and country ambiguously in flux. Fortunately for the contemporary audience, Juan Rana did not suffer the same fate as the doomed Hapsburg Empire. Indeed, Juan Rana's ambiguous and amphibolic acting, based on the most part on his gayness, still enjoys the last laugh.

Considering that historically, a gay man typically represents the ills of traditional society and, for many, is a bad omen for the future of said society, the long-lived popularity of the Juan Rana person/persona must be considered compellingly rare and captivatingly complex. This is even more remarkable for a once ultra-Catholic Spain, where its medieval literature 'linked male homosexuality with Islam or religious nonconformity ... The perceived association between Islam and homosexuality was strengthened as the Crusades and the reconquest of Spain brought Christians into protracted conflict with the Arab World' (Greenberg 268). Surely, homosexuality remained, at least in the Spanish unconscious, connected to the enemy, the infidel, the invader that was ultimately driven out. Indeed, in Christian terms

[h]istorically, the representation of sodomy has been marked by nothing so much as sodomy's troubled relationship to representation itself. Repre-

sented as unrepresentable, named as that which cannot be named, sodomy is *peccatum ilud horribile, inter christianos non nominandum* – the horrible crime not to be named among Christians ... (MacFarlane 25)

Juan Rana and all that his life and work involved and stood for demand a rethinking of baroque limits of permissiveness and homogeneity. Those who wrote and produced his plays and his many fans from all walks of life must also be considered his coproducers of gay and subversive meaning. Ultimately, this theory means that a vast majority of a largely urban baroque Spanish society were in collusion with the Juan Rana person/persona. As such, we cannot underestimate the enormity of the Juan Rana phenomenon from a theatrical and societal point of view.

The enormity of the Juan Rana phenomenon must also be put into context from a logistical standpoint. David Higgs laments that '[a]n account of homosexuality in a city established through contemporary oral history gained from willing and loquacious informants is not available to the historian of earlier times. A narrative has frequently to be constructed out of mere scraps of information' (5). Obviously this is not the case with the Juan Rana *entremeses*. Instead of scraps of information, the over fifty Juan Rana *entremeses* correspond to an extraordinary body of evidence. Scott Bravmann, in coming to terms with previous attempts at writing gay history, also comments that

> historical truths – the strategic lessons to be drawn from history – might well be approached through a literary historiography that draws on the dissolution of the distinction between realistic and fictional representations as proposed by recent theories of discourse and locates 'factual' as well as 'subjective' truths in the ways we understand, interpret, and write about the past. (29)

In this sense, the Juan Rana *entremeses* represent an important means for better understanding society and homosexuality in baroque Spain. The numerous *entremeses* are undoubtedly an extraordinary 'subjective truth' to add to the 'factual.'

Factually, what must be remembered is Juan Rana's physiognomy, station, and status in baroque Spain. Firstly, his onstage presence while undoubtedly larger than life cannot be considered ominous or menacing. As a short and pudgy actor he can easily be perceived as not much of a man at all. While obviously a privileged actor he nonetheless held a marginalized position in society because of his profession. As a buffoon he was freer than most actors to act out his foolishness and weaknesses and Juan Rana was already labelled and well known as a gay man following his arrest. As such, when the actor played up the irregular and the unnatural in his many *entremeses* he represented no threat to those who witnessed his antics; Juan Rana was a nonthreatening physical, societal, and sexual entity. These theatrical and life circumstances, along with a great shift and slippage of the male construct and society itself, created a unique environment for the engendering of the Juan Rana phenomenon. Juan Rana's life and career represent a unique opportunity to generate a compelling 'dissolution of the distinction between realistic and fictional representations' of homosexuality in the Spanish baroque period.

Notes

1 What's in a Name?

1 A portion of this chapter has previously appeared as 'Juan Rana, A Gay Golden Age *Gracioso*.'
2 All definitions are from the 1726 edition of the *Diccionario de Autoridades*, unless otherwise specified.
3 All translations are by the author and Marla Arbach.
4 Dates supplied for all *entremeses* of this study refer to date of publication and not of performance. It can be assumed that the majority of the *entremeses* were performed between 1636 (the date of Juan Rana's arrest) and 1658 when Juan Rana is said to have 'retired.' He did, of course, return to the stage after 1658, especially for command performances. His appearance in 1672 in *El triunfo de Juan Rana*, an *entremés* which will be analysed in chapter 2, is a case in point.
5 For more information on Juan Rana's *commedia dell'arte* connection, see Sáez Raposo.
6 The adjective *sayagués* refers to a person from the Sayago County of the province of Zamora and figuratively implies someone of coarse and uneducated background. In Golden Age literature, it became a topos for all rustic speak and specifically in drama it was used to typify rural characters (*Diccionario de la lengua española, Real Academia Española*).
7 For further reading on the *pecado nefando* see Perry, Saint-Säens, and Tomás y Valiente.
8 For more discussion of their interpretations, see Thompson, 'Juan Rana, A Gay Golden Age *Gracioso*' 240–3. See also Cartagena-Calderón for an excellent summary of the critical response to Juan Rana's *pecado nefando* mask (166).

9 For further discussion on various *entremeses* written after Juan Rana's arrest, particularly those of Quiñones de Benavente, see Thompson, 'Juan Rana, A Gay Golden Age *Gracioso*,' and 'Crossing the Gendered "Clothes"-Line.'

10 Belmonte Bermúdez was born in Seville in approximately 1587. His youthful adventures in the New World were the subject of his first play, *Algunas hazañas de las muchas de don García Hurtado de Mendoza, Marqués de Cañete*, written in collaboration with eight other *ingenios* in 1622. Belmonte Bermúdez also wrote various poems around this time, some of which were praised by Lope de Vega. In 1649 Gerónimo Cáncer y Velasco, an important literary personage and *entremesista* of the period, made a *vejámen* or burlesque speech about Belmonte Bermúdez to the *Academia Castellana Matritense*. This shows that in the mid-century Belmonte Bermúdez was to be found in Madrid. Belmonte Bermúdez is, perhaps, best known today for his play *El mayor contrario amigo y Diablo predicador*, which in the nineteenth-century was included in Ramón Mesonero Romano's *Biblioteca de Autores españoles* along with his *La Renegada de Valladolid*. Importantly, this author wrote collaborative plays with Moreto, Calderón, and Rojas Zorrilla (La Barrera y Leirado 28–30).

2 The Self-'Reflective' Juan Rana

1 This tribute appears in *El triunfo de Juan Rana*, the first *entremés* studied in this chapter. Calderón is, of course, one of the most revered playwrights of seventeenth-century Spain. His plays include *La dama duende* (1629), *El médico de su honra* (1637), and his best known works, *La vida es sueño* (1635) and *El alcalde de Zalamea* (1637). As the dates of his plays indicate, Calderón enjoyed great success up to the 1640s. During the period 1644–9, however, successive theatre closures combined with personal problems caused a decline in his literary output. Ordained as a priest in 1651, Calderón moved to Toledo where he dedicated much of his writing to *autos sacramentales*. In 1666, three years after his return to Madrid, he was named the royal chaplain. Phillip IV's death in 1665, however, caused further theatre closures. It was not until 1672 that court plays resumed with Calderón's *Fieras afemina amor*, the play in which *El triunfo de Juan Rana* is inserted. Two years prior to his death in 1681 Juan Rana was awarded a pension from Charles II to supplement his meagre earnings (Rodríguez and Tordera 9–12).

2 For Esther Menaker, the double and the *Doppelgänger* are not synonymous: 'Double is inevitably an inadequate translation of the Dopplegänger, which contains a somewhat mystical meaning. It is compounded with the German verb "to go" (literally, "double goer"), and therefore implies a more active

quality than the English noun "double" can convey' (91). Her differentiation between the two terms confirms the need to use double and *Doppelgänger* as distinct analytical entities.

3 *El triunfo de Juan Rana* is one of the few *entremeses* in this study that has been directly linked with its corresponding main play. This linking has allowed for a greater analysis of both plays. Further research is needed to rejoin the other *entremeses* with their main play siblings.

4 For more information on Juan Rana, see Thompson, 'Juan Rana, A Gay Golden Age *Gracioso*'; 'Crossing the Gendered "Clothes"-Line'; and 'Fencing and Fornication in Calderón's *El desafío de Juan Rana.*'

5 Greer and Varey include a letter sent by Lord Sunderland to Lord Arlington which describes a first-hand account of the *Fieras* production (25).

6 Many critics believe the premiere of *Fieras afemina amor* took place in January 1670 but investigation has shown that the play was not staged until January of 1672. This date change is significant for this study as it shows that Juan Rana died soon after his performance in *El triunfo*. For further information concerning the research of the final date of *Fieras* production, see Greer and Varey 34–5.

7 See Wilson (23) for an overview of the typical depiction of Hercules as hero during this period. In reference to the introduction of *Fieras*, Don W. Cruickshank oversaw the posthumous publication of Wilson's edition of the play. Cruickshank also wrote sections I and II of the introduction, while Wilson wrote section III, 'Calderón's Ignoble Hercules' (23–46). In light of this, although Cruickshank contributed to the introduction, we will cite Wilson as the author. For further explanation, see the preface to *Fieras* (vii–ix).

8 Three examples of Juan Rana's cross-dressing *entremeses* are *La boda de Juan Rana* (Cáncer y Velasco), *Juan Rana muger* (Cáncer y Velasco), and *El parto de Juan Rana* (Lanini y Sagredo). The cross-dressing Juan Rana will be studied in more depth in chapter 3.

9 See chapter 3 for further discussion of the prowomen message that many Juan Rana *entremeses* present.

10 This is an excellent example of the many gender-bending representations by the Juan Rana persona which will be considered in chapter 3. Here, however, it is not through cross-dressing that gender-bending is achieved but rather through a female representation of his soul.

11 Wilson, in note 1454 of his critical edition, explains that Antonio de Escamilla was a famous *gracioso* who was a contemporary of Juan Rana. On many occasions, as seen in lists of actors, both acted together. For further information on this actor, see Hannah Bergman's study of Quiñones de Benavente, 475–6.

12 According to La Barrera y Leirado, Moreto y Cavana was born in Madrid in 1618 into a family of Italian origin dedicated to commerce. He studied at Alcalá de Henares, graduating in 1639. He showed literary promise and, indeed, '[s]u ingenio, viveza y natural festivo, le abrieron las puertas de los saraos y academias, y acaso debió al jóven é ilustre Calderón la entrada y parte que tuvo en los festines literarios del Buen Retiro' (275) (his intelligence, vivacity, and gregarious nature opened the doors to important gatherings and societies, and in fact, it was to the young and illustrious Calderón that he owed his acceptance and role in the literary banquets of the Buen Retiro). In 1649 he became a member of the *Academia de Madrid ó Castellana* and, importantly, the secretary of this organization was Cáncer y Velasco, his dramatic collaborator. There would seem, however, to have been a great turnabout in the latter years of the playwright's life. He became a priest in Toledo and 'renunciados los aplausos que le daban merecidamente los teatros, consagró su pluma á las alabanzas divinas, convertidos el entusiasmo ó furor poético en espíritu de devocion' (renouncing the much-deserved plaudits he got from the theatre, he dedicated his pen to praising God, and converted his enthusiasm or poetic fervour into a spirit of devotion). He died in Toledo in 1662 (275–6). For further information on Moreto's life and work, see Castañeda.

13 The *Doppelgänger* fits many literary movements and periods as Andrew J. Webber explains: 'It represents the subject as more or less pathologically divided between reality and fantasy ... As such the figure can be seen to gauge the shifting relations between realist and fantastic tendencies in writing spanning the ages of Classicism, Romanticism, Realism, Naturalism and Modernism' (1). This would seem to describe the interludes written for Juan Rana and, in this way, 'Baroquism' should be added to this list of 'isms.'

14 Celia E. Weller Richmond writes that '[i]n many senses, *La tragicomedia de Calisto y Melibea* (1499) by Fernando de Rojas, a work popularly known as *La Celestina*, exemplifies the strict moral tone and temper of the times in Spain. It concerns two noble lovers, Calisto and Melibea, who resort to the services of a go-between named Celestina to further their love. The lives of these three characters become entangled through a variety of comic mistakes and beguilements, and in the end all three are brought to disaster.

   The Celestina presents the reader with a number of contradictions. The work cautions individuals who are blinded by love and advises them against the deceits of go-betweens and immoral servants. At the same time, *The Celestina* seems to celebrate human diversity, accepting existence as a complex set of natural impulses – some noble and generous, others base and egotistical. Even its original title, *La tragicomedia*, indicates that *The Celestina* is neither tragedy nor comedy, but both. Its structure is that of a novel in dialogue form; this structure illustrates the tensions between the form of the novel and the form of the drama. It also illustrates tension between tragedy and comedy and between the idealism of the lovers and the materialism of the servants. The literary sources of this work are Latin and medieval, but *The Celestina* also expresses a vision of life that diverges from the spirit of the Middle Ages and propels Spanish literature into the Renaissance.'

Eugenio Asensio states that '*La Celestina*, en lo que podríamos llamar el piso de los criados, y la novela picaresca en todo su ámbito han fecundado el entremés' (29) (the *Celestina*, in what could be called the strength of its servant-class characters, and the picaresque novel as a whole, have enriched the *entremés*). *Los dos Juan Ranas* as a parody of original work has more than just a thematic debt to the famous tragicomedy.

15 Later in his career Rank returns to the subject of the double motif, stating that the Western form of tragedy has its roots in Greek cults and rituals. Here the 'commoner' became temporarily united 'with irrational life-forces from which the average man in his daily existence had to be protected by all sorts of tabus.' But on festive occasions the priests and kings lifted these taboos – 'It is from such seasonal renewal of the irrational self in the spiritual ceremonies of magic participation that culture developed' (*Beyond Psychology* 83–4). Rank is, therefore, connecting the double with the irrational aspects of life that are celebrated during carnival time. Rank's double theory agrees with the theory that the carnivalesque *entremés* is a temporary celebration of the irrational and of the lifting of societal rules and taboos.

16 La Barrera y Leirado informs us that Cáncer y Velasco was born into a family of noble lineage at the end of the sixteenth century and died in 1655. His talent was well suited to the *entremés* considering '[s]obresalió Cáncer en los versos de donaire, si bien prodigó en ellos demasiado los equívocos, y los afeó con retruécanos de mal gusto' (62) (Cáncer excelled in witty verses, although he peppered them with too much double-talk and spoiled them with vulgarity). La Barrera y Leirado's condemning tone in this quotation reflects the era's puritanical stance on the equivocally lurid. Cáncer wrote various plays in conjunction with Calderón, Moreto, Luis Vélez, Matos, Zabalesta, and others while penning on his own only two burlesque *comedias*. La Barrera y Leirado notes that *Juan Ranilla* appeared in *Verjel de entremeses y conceptos del donaire*, Zaragoza, 1675. The text used here, however, comes from *Rasgos del ocio*.

17 This would seem to be an ironic reference to the last scene in Tirso de Molina's *El burlador de Sevilla*, where the dead father appears as an avenging statue.

18 This is but one of three Juan Rana *entremeses* where the portrait is used as a theatrical device, as Laura Bass has shown. In her study of *El retrato vivo* (Moreto), *El retrato de Juan Rana* (Solís), and *El retrato de Juan Rana* (Villaviciosa), she shows that these three *entremeses* 'offer a privileged window onto the complex dynamics of the social center and margins in the Spain of the later Habsburgs' (2). In this study I concentrate on Villaviciosa's *entremés*. I would like to thank the author for sharing her paper with me.

19 This *entremés* alludes to the fop/*mujer varonil* (or weak/feminine man) and strong/masculine woman relation described by Gail Bradbury. Bradbury's engaging argument concerning this Golden Age phenomenon is discussed in chapter 3.

20 In *El parto de Juan Rana*, analysed in chapter 3, the 'dramatic' birth of another Juan Ranilla is a more fantastical gender-bending representation.

21 Huerta Calvo notes that 'el engaño de los ojos,' the most classic motif of the *entremés*, originated in Eastern literary tradition and was first introduced into Spanish literature by Juan Manuel (23). Of course, when speaking of painting as a means to 'pull the wool over the eyes' of the gullible, Cervantes' *El retablo de maravillas* immediately comes to mind.

22 Hannah E. Bergman in *Ramillete de entremeses y bailes nuevamente escogidos de los antiguos poetas de España siglo XVII* (1970), affirms that this *entremés* was penned by Moreto: 'Apareció *el entremés de la loa de Juan Rana* impreso por primera vez en 1664, a nombre de Moreto, en *Rasgos del ocio, segunda parte*, de donde la copiamos. Volvió a estamparse como obra de D. Francisco de Avellaneda ... en las colecciones *Floresta de entremeses* (Madrid, 1691) y *Manojito de entremeses* (Pamplona, 1700), sin otro cambio. También se conserva en manuscrito anónimo en la Biblioteca Nacional (Ms. 16.748)' (429) (*La loa de Juan Rana* was first printed in 1664 and attributed to Moreto, in *Rasgos del ocio*, part 2, from where we have taken the text. It was later published attributed to D. Francisco de Avellaneda ... in the collections *Floresta de entremeses* (Madrid, 1691), and *Manojito de entremeses* (Pamplona, 1700), with no other change. It also exists as anonymous manuscript 16.748 in the Biblioteca Nacional de España). See note 12 of this chapter for biographical information on Moreto.

23 The use of the frame as a means to create an illusion is much like Cervantes' *El retablo de maravillas*, where a whole village is tricked into seeing, within a frame, pictures that are not there.

24 The full text of this *entremés* reads: 'Ya en Olmedo, señores,/ Rana se ha

vuelto,/ el galán de la loa,/ la flor de Olmedo' (437) (Already in Olmedo, gentlemen,/ Rana has become,/ the hero of the *loa*,/ the flower of Olmedo). This passage sung by musicians refers to a popular Spanish song: 'Esta noche le mataron/ al Caballero, la gala de Medina, la flor de Olmedo' (Tonight they murdered/ the nobleman, the jewel of Medina, the flower of Olmedo). This *cantar* is supposedly based on the death of Juan de Vivero in 1521 (Rico 13). It was, of course, Lope de Vega's *El caballero de Olmedo* (1620) that made this legend theatrically famous. In Lope de Vega's play, the famous *seguidilla* (refrain) is also sung but 'desde lejos en el vestuario, y véngase acercando la voz, como que camina' (197) (from far offstage, and the voice gets closer as if it were approaching). This singing approach mimics the advance of Alonso's impending death, the foreboding message of the verses. In *La loa de Juan Rana*, however, the singers mockingly note that the actor has become Olmedo. To their musical mockery, Juan Rana replies: 'Pues escuchad: yo confieso/ que casi me parecía/ que yo podía ser Olmedo/ así en algunas cosillas' (437) (Listen: I admit/ that it almost seemed to me/ that I could be Olmedo/ in some small way). Indeed, with his arrest for *el pecado nefando*, Juan Rana could have been put to death. Instead he, unlike Alonso, returned alive and well from *la Puerta de Alcalá*.

25 The importance of Lope de Vega's theatrical treatise as it relates to the Juan Rana *entremeses* is a focal point of chapter 4.

3 Crossing the Gendered 'Clothes'-Line

1 A portion of this chapter has previously appeared as 'Crossing the Gendered "Clothes"-Line.'

2 See Velasco chapter 4, Cartagena-Calderón, and Vélez Quiñones.

3 For biographical information see page 165, note 16. The version used here of this *entremés* is taken from *Floresta de entremeses, y rasgos del ocio a diferentes assumptos, de bayles, y mogigangas*, Madrid, 1691.

4 The work of Cáncer y Velasco was continuously censored in this period. One such censored case was his *Los putos*. In this *entremés* a young man, madly in love with a woman who pays him no heed, seeks out the aid of a witch. The magical document that she gives him makes anyone who reads it fall violently in love and lust for the young man. Intended for the eyes of his beloved, it is read, however, by a series of male officials. Each reacts in the prescribed manner exalting the beauty of the young man and his alluring body parts. It is no wonder that Cáncer y Velasco 'sería uno de los entremesistas más afamados de la centuria' (Huerta Calvo 228) (was one of the most infamous *entremesistas* of the century).

5 This is precisely the use of the *guardainfante*, the central leitmotif of Quiñones de Benavente's *El guardainfante I y II.*

6 Only at the singing conclusion of *Juan Rana muger* is he identified as mayor (161). Obviously, the persona is so well known that his office is taken for granted.

7 *Barbas* is also the name of the stock old man character in a typical theatrical company in this period.

8 Nicky Hart states, 'The best indicator of the material burdens of procreative labor in the pre-modern era is the diminished vitality of the female of the species. Before the modern era, excess female mortality was normal' (10).

9 La Barrera y Leirado notes that the first bibliographical mention of Lanini y Sagredo dates from the late 1660s. In 1668 'sazonados entremeses' (provocative *entremeses*) by Lanini appear in *La ociosidad entretenida*. *El Ramillete de sainetes* (1672) and *Flor de entremeses* (1676) also include works by this author. Significantly, his play *Juana de Jesus María* was banned in its entirety by the Inquisition (200). In 1685 Lanini was a play censor and documentation shows that he continued to exercise this privilege up to 1706. *El parto de Juan Rana* exists only in manuscript form and does not carry a date. It is not mentioned in La Barrera y Leirado's list of Lanini's works. We can only surmise that it was not in the best interest of an official censor to have his name publicly associated with an *entremés* of such a 'scandalous' nature.

10 This physical imprisonment of Juan Rana is in opposition to his 'inverted' and figurative entrapment in the 'body' of a maiden bound by the rules of patriarchal tyranny seen in *Juan Rana muger.*

11 See Velasco for further information on male pregnancy in the baroque era.

4 'Mas apetezco fuentes que braseros'

1 A portion of this chapter has previously appeared as 'Fencing and Fornication in Calderón's *El desafío de Juan Rana.*'

2 For further historical detail, see Velasco, chapter 4, 'The Fear of Metrosexuality in Early Modern Spain,' and Cartagena-Calderón.

3 Brian Dutton had shared the poem in question with John T. Cull and the latter cites this with gratitude (40 note 3). No bibliographical reference to Dutton's work on the poem in question is available.

4 While Juan Rana repeats the adjectives *recto* and *firme* used by his wife, he replaces *perfilado* with *afilado*. While this lexical change consistent with Juan Rana's bumbling mask would seem slight, there could be seen an allusion to *alfiler*. As Frédéric Serralta has shown, '[A]lusión al alfiler como símbolo de la homosexualidad masculina, ya bastante clara de por sí, no era por lo visto

excepcional en el teatro cómico de entonces' (84) (Allusions to *alfiler* as a symbol of male homosexuality, already quite clear, were apparently not exceptional in the comic theatre of the period). The pejorative use of *alfiler* will be discussed later in this chapter in the analysis of *Los muertos vivos*.

5   Herrera's *Diccionario español de textos médicos antiguos* gives a series of medical references to the term *opilación* and *opilar* that indicate this malady as a blockage or obstruction of evacuative orifices.

6   Rodríguez and Tordera have used for their edition of this *entremés* the text published in *Tardes*, 1663 fols. 27v–32r but cite an alternative text from the Barcelona and Seville versions of the *entremés*:

> RANA: Espere usted un poco,
> iré yo por la merienda.
>
> PARRA: ¿Qué es lo que dice? ¿Está loco?
> Yo sólo vengo a reñir.
>
> RANA: Es que ando buscando modo
> para darle a usted un bocado
> con un manjar muy sabroso,
> porque muera usted comiendo.
>
> PARRA: Saque la espada o me corro.
>
> RANA: Wait a minute,
> I'll go and get the picnic lunch.
>
> PARRA: What are you talking about? Are you crazy?
> I've only come to fight.
>
> RANA: It's that I've been trying to
> poison you
> with a good-tasting delicacy,
> so that you die eating.
>
> PARRA: Draw your sword or I'll run away.

This text is also quite suggestive for its sexual subtext, if we consider that *correr* also means the running of a liquid, an obvious reference to ejaculation.

7   In the case of *Los muertos vivos*, the original *Joco Seria* text is used. Bergman explains that the collection was a late work of the author (74).

8   The version of *El mundo al revés* used here is from Cotarelo y Mori's collection, 746–8. Cotarelo y Mori has included all three variants of the text in his collection.

9   The version of *Las fiestas del aldea* used here is found in Javier Huerta Calvo's edition listed in the bibliography.

10   This entremés does not appear in the author's famous collection *Joco Seria*

but rather exists as a handwritten manuscript in the Biblioteca Nacional de España (MS 15105).

11 Salvador here refers to Jaime Salvador, Juan Rana's 'straight' man (Bergman 544).

12 *Salsa* which appeared earlier in the text, is also a term used for semen (Alzieu et al. 167, poem 90, 1.42). While this interpretation of the *salsa* is less easily substantiated, it is nonetheless an interesting concurrence.

13 There is some discussion concerning the exact wording in these two lines. Bergman notes that Cotarelo believes that the first 'quemo' is perhaps 'extremo,' making the line read, 'I am extremely in love.' On the other hand, she suggests that the second 'quemo' is an error for 'temo,' making the line read, 'This is what I fear' (521). We have, however, kept the original version of the text, which repeats 'quemo.'

14 The version of *Las fiestas del aldea* used here is found in Javier Huerta Calvo's edition listed in the bibliography.

Bibliography

Primary Sources

Belmonte Bermúdez, Luis de. '*Una rana hace ciento.*' *Flor de entremeses y sainetes de diferentes autores* (1657). 2nd ed. Madrid: Imprenta de Fortanet, 1903. 183–205.

Bernardo de Quirós, Francisco. '*Las fiestas del Aldea.*' *Teatro breve de los siglos XVI y XVII: Entremeses, loas, bailes, jácaras y mojigangas.* Ed. Javier Huerta Calvo. Madrid: Taurus, 1985. 235–42.

Calderón de la Barca, Pedro. '*El desafío de Juan Rana.*' *Entremeses y jácaras y mojigangas.* Ed. Evangelina Rodríguez and Antonio Tordera. Madrid: Castalia, 1982. 200–13.

– '*El triunfo de Juan Rana.*' *Fieras afemina amor.* Ed. Edward M. Wilson. Kassel: Reichenberger, 1984. 113–22.

Cáncer y Velasco, Gerónimo de. '*La boda de Juan Rana.*' *Floresta de entremeses, y rasgos del ocio a diferentes assumptos, de bayles, y mogigangas.* Madrid: Antonio de Zafra, 1691. 145–57.

– '*Juan Rana muger.*' *Flor de entremeses, bayles, y loas: Escogidos de los mejores Ingenios de España.* Zaragoza: Impresor del Hospital de nuestra Seña de Gracia, 1666. 154–62.

– *Juan Ranilla. Rasgos del ocio, en diferentes bayles, entremeses, y loas de diversos autores.* Part 2. Madrid: Biblioteca Nacional de España, 1664. 210–24.

Lanini y Sagredo, Francisco Pedro. *El parto de Juan Rana.* 14.089-43, Madrid: Biblioteca Nacional de España, MS. fol. 426v-35

Moreto y Cavana, Agustín. '*Los dos Juan Ranas.*' *Vergel de entremeses.* Ed. Jesús Cañedo Fernandez. Madrid: Consejo Superior de Investigaciones Científicas, Instituto 'Miguel de Cervantes,' 1970. 27–44.

– '*La loa de Juan Rana.*' *Ramillete de entremeses y bailes nuevamente recogidos de los antiguos poetas de España siglo XVII.* Ed. Hannah E. Bergman. Madrid: Clásicos Castalia, 1970. 429–40.

Quiñones de Benavente, Luis. '*Los muertos vivos.*' *Joco Seria. Burlas veras, o reprehensión moral, y festiva de los desordenes públicos: En doze entremeses representados, y viente y quatro cantados.* Valladolid: Juan Antolin de Lago, 1653. Fol: 226–33.

– '*El mundo.*' *Colección de entremeses, loas, bailes, jácaras y mojigangas desde fines del siglo XVI a mediados del XVIII.* Ed. Emilio Cortarelo y Mori. Tomo I. Vol. 2. Madrid: Casa Editorial Bailly/Baillière, 1911. 831–2.

– *El mundo al revés. Colección de entremeses, loas, bailes, jácaras y mojigangas desde fines del siglo XVI a mediados del XVIII.* Ed. Emilio Cortarelo y Mori. Tomo I. Vol. 2. Madrid: Casa Editorial Bailly/Baillière, 1911. 746–8.

– *El pipote en nombre de Juan Rana.* Madrid: Biblioteca de España. MS. 15105. fols 14–18.

– '*El soldado.*' *Joco Seria. Burlas veras, o reprehensión moral, y festiva de los desordenes públicos: En doze entremeses representados, y veinte y quatro cantados.* Valladolid: Juan Antolin de Lago, 1653. Fols 218–21.

Villaviciosa, Sebastián de. '*El retrato de Juan Rana. Tardes apacibles de gustoso entretenimiento, repartidas en varios entremeses, y bayles entremesados, escogidos de los mejores Ingenios de España.* Madrid: Biblioteca Nacional de España, MS. R8251. 1663. fols 52v-57.

Secondary Sources

Aguirre, Manuel. 'The Evolution of Dreams.' *Neohelicon.* 17.2 (1990): 9–26.

Alzieu, Pierre, Robert Jammes, and Yvan Lissorgues, eds. *Poesía erótica del Siglo de Oro.* Barcelona: Editorial Crítica, 1983.

Alemán, Mateo. *Guzmán de Alfarache I.* Ed. José María Micó. Madrid: Cátedra, 2001.

Arellano, I., J.M. Escudero, and A. Madroñal, eds. *Entremeses completos I: Jocoseria* by Luis Quiñones de Benavente. Madrid: Universidad de Navarra, Editorial Iberoamericana, 2001.

Asensio, Eugenio. *Itinerario del entremés desde Lope de Rueda a Quiñones de Benavente.* Madrid: Gredos, 1965.

Bass, Laura. 'Framing the Margins on Center Stage: The Portrait *Entremeses* of Juan Rana.' Annual Meeting of the Renaissance Society of America, Toronto, 2003.

Bakhtin, Mikhail. *Rabelais and His World.* Trans. Hélène Iswolsky. Bloomingdale: Indiana UP, 1984.

Bergman, Hannah E. *Luis Quiñones de Benavente y sus entremeses: Con un catálogo biográfico de los autores citados en sus obras.* Madrid: Castalia, 1965.

– 'Introducción crítica.' *Ramillete de entremeses y bailes nuevamente recogido de los antiguos poetas de España siglo XVII*. Ed. Hannah E. Beryman. Madrid: Castalia, 1970. 9–52.

Bergson, Henri. 'Laughter.' *Comedy*. Ed. Wylie Sypher. New York: Doubleday and Anchor Books, 1956. 59–190.

Bersani, Leo. 'Is the Rectum a Grave?' Reprinted in *Reclaiming Sodom*. Ed. Jonathan Goldberg. 249–64. New York: Routledge, 1994.

Bradbury, Gail. 'Irregular Sexuality in the Spanish "Comedia."' *Modern Language Review* 76 (1981): 566–80.

Bravmann, Scott. *Queer Fictions of the Past: History, Culture and Difference*. Cambridge: Cambridge UP, 1997.

Bullough, Vern L., and Bonnie Bullough. *Cross Dressing, Sex and Gender*. Philadelphia: U of Pennsylvania P, 1993.

Butler, Judith. *Bodies that Matter: On the Discursive Limits of 'Sex.'* New York: Routledge, 1993.

– *Gender Trouble: Feminism and the Subversion of Identity*. New York: Routledge, 1990.

– 'Imitation and Gender Insubordination.' *Inside/out: Lesbian Theories, Gay Theories*. Ed. Diana Fuss. New York: Routledge, 1991. 13–31.

Calderwood, James L. *To Be Or Not to Be: Negation and Metadrama in* Hamlet. New York: Columbia UP, 1983.

Cartagena-Calderón, José. '"Él es tan rara persona." Sobre cortesanos, lindos, sodomitas y otras masculinidades de la temprana Edad Moderna.' *Lesbianism and Homosexuality in Early Modern Spain: Literature and Theater in Context*. Ed. María José Delgado and Alain Saint-Saens. New Orleans, LA: UP of the South, 2000. 139–75.

Carrasco, Rafael. *Inquisición y repression sexual en Valencia: Historia de los sodomitas (1565–1785)*. Barcelona: Laertes, 1985.

Castañeda, James L. *Agustín Moreto*. New York: Twayne, 1974.

Castiglione, Baltasar de. *El cortesano*. Trad. Juan Boscán. [1534]. Ed. Rogelio Reyes Cano. Madrid: Espasa-Calpe, 1984.

Cirlot, Juan Eduardo. *A Dictionary of Symbols*. Trans. Jack Sage. New York: Philosophical Library, 1981.

Cela, Camilo José. *Diccionario secreto*. Madrid: Alianza, 1968.

Connor (Swietlicki), Catherine. 'The *Preceptistas* and Beyond: Spectators Making "Meanings" in the *Corral de Comedias*.' Hispania 82 (September, 1999): 417–28.

Cotarelo y Mori, Emilio. Introduction. *Colección de entremeses, loas, bailes, jácaras y mojigangas desde fines del siglo XVI a mediados del XVIII*. Ed. Emilio Cotarelo y Mori. Tomo I. Vol. 1. Madrid: Casa Editorial Bailly/Baillière, 1911. i–clxiii.

Covarrubias Orozco, Sebastián de. *Tesoro de la lengua castellana o española*. Ed. Felipe C.R. Maldonado. Madrid: Castalia, 1995.

Cull, John T. 'The "Knight of the Broken Lance" and His "Trusty Steed": On Don Quixote and Rocinante.' *Cervantes* 10.2 (fall, 1900): 37–53.

Curtius, Ernst Robert. *European Literature and the Latin Middle Ages.* Trans. Willard R. Trask. Princeton UP, 1990.

de Armas, Frederick A. 'The Critical Tower.' *The Prince in the Tower: Perceptions of La vida es sueño.* Ed. Frederick A. de Armas. Lewisburg: Bucknell UP, 1993. 3–14.

Diccionario de Autoridades. Real Academia Española. Madrid: Gredos, 1990.

Ekins, Richard. *Male Femaling: A Grounded Theory Approach to Cross-Dressing and Sex-Changing.* New York: Routledge, 1997.

Epstein, Julia, and Kristina Straub. 'Introduction: The Guarded Body.' *Body Guards: The Cultural Politics of Gender Ambiguity.* Ed. Julia Epstein and Kristina Straub. New York: Routledge, 1991. 1–28.

Ferris, Lesley. 'Introduction: Current Crossings.' *Crossing the Stage: Controversies of Cross-Dressing.* Ed. Lesley Ferris. New York: Routledge, 1993. 1–19.

Ford, Andrew. 'Katharsis: The Ancient Problem.' *Performance and Performativity.* Ed. Eve Kosofsky Sedgewick and Andrew Parker. New York: Routledge, 1995. 109–32.

Fuss, Diana. 'Inside/Out.' *Inside/Out: Lesbian and Gay Theories.* Ed. Diana Fuss. New York: Routledge, 1991. 1–10.

Freud, Sigmund. 'The Uncanny.' *The Standard Edition of the Complete Psychological Works of Sigmund Freud.* Vol. 17. London: Hogarth, 1955. 217–52.

Friedländer, Max J. *Landscape, Portrait, Still-Life: Their Origin and Development.* Trans. R.F.C. Hull. Oxford: Bruno Cassirer, 1949.

Garber, Marjorie. *Vested Interests: Cross-Dressing and Cultural Anxiety.* New York: Routledge, 1992.

Goldberg, Jonathan. *Sodometrics: Renaissance Texts, Modern Sexualities.* Stanford: Stanford UP, 1992.

Girard, René. *Essays on Literature, Mimesis, and Anthropology. 'To double business bound.'* Baltimore: Johns Hopkins UP, 1978.

Greenberg, David F. *The Construction of Homosexuality.* Chicago: U of Chicago P, 1998.

Greer, Margaret Rich, and J.E. Varey. *El teatro palaciego en Madrid: Estudio y documentos.* Madrid: Támesis, 1997.

Grimal, Pierre. *The Dictionary of Classical Mythology.* Trans. A.R. Maxwell-Hyslop. Cambridge, MA: Blackwell, 1996.

Guerard, Albert J., ed. *Stories of the Double.* Philadelphia: Lippincott, 1967.

Hamilton, Marybeth. '"I'm the Queen of the Bitches": Female Impersonation and Mae West's *Pleasure Man.' Crossing the Stage: Controversies on Cross-Dressing.* Ed. Lesley Ferris. New York: Routledge, 1993. 107–19.

Hart, Nicky. 'Procreation: The Substance of Female Oppression in Modern Society.' *Debating Gender, Debating Sexuality.* Ed. Nikki R. Keddie. New York: New York UP, 1996. 5–48.

Herrera, María Teresa. *Diccionario español de textos médicos antiguos.* Madrid: Arco/Libros, 1996.

Higgs, David. Introduction. *Queer Sites: Gay Urban Histories Since 1600.* Ed. David Higgs. New York: Routledge, 1999. 1–9.

Howard, Jean E. 'Cross-Dressing, the Theater, and Gender Struggle in Early Modern England.' *Cross Dressing: Sex and Gender.* Ed. Vern L. Bullough and Bonnie Bullough. Philadelphia: U of Pennsylvania P, 1993.

Huerta Calvo, Javier. *Teatro breve de los siglos XVI y XVII: Entremeses, loas, bailes, jácaras y mojigangas.* Madrid: Taurus, 1985.

Keppler, Carl Francis. *The Literature of the Second Self.* Tucson: U of Arizona P, 1972.

Keddie, Nikki R. *Debating Gender, Debating Sexuality.* New York: New York UP, 1996.

La Barrera y Leirado, Cayetano Alberto de. *Catálogo bibliográfico y biográfico del teatro antiguo español, desde sus orígenes hasta mediados del siglo XVIII.* Facsimiles ed. Madrid: Gredos, 1969.

Lacan, Jacques. *Écrits.* Trans. Alan Sheridan. New York: Norton, 1977.

Lévi-Strauss, Claude, 'The Principles of Kinship.' *The Elementary Structures of Kinship.* Boston: Beacon, 1969.

Lobato, María Luisa. 'Un actor en Palacio: Felipe IV escribe sobre Juan Rana.' *Cuadernos de Historia Moderna* 23.V (1999): 79–111.

MacFarlane, Cameron. *The Sodomite in Fiction and Satire, 1660–1775.* New York: Columbia UP, 1997.

Martín, Adrienne L. 'Rereading *El amante liberal* in the Age of Contrapuntal Sexualities.' *Cervantes and His Postmodern Constituencies.* Ed. Anne J. Cruz and Carroll B. Johnson. New York: Garland, 1998. 151–69.

McKendrick, Melveena. *Theatre in Spain 1400–1700.* Cambridge: Cambridge UP, 1989.

Melchior-Bonnet, Sabine. *The Mirror: A History.* Trans Katharine H. Jewett. New York: Routledge. 2001.

Menaker, Esther. *Otto Rank, a Rediscovered Legacy.* New York: Columbia UP, 1982.

Moreto, Agustín. *El lindo don Diego.* Ed. Víctor García Ruiz. Madrid: Espasa-Calpe, 1993.

Norman, Larry F. 'The Theatrical Baroque.' *The Theatrical Baroque.* Chicago: David and Alfred Smart Museum of Art, U of Chicago, 2001. 1–11.

Pérez Escohotado, Javier. *Sexo e inquisición en España.* Madrid: Temas de Hoy, 1992.

Perry, Mary Elizabeth. 'The "Nefarious Sin" in Early Modern Seville.' *The Pursuit of Sodomy: Male Homosexuality in Renaissance and Enlightenment Europe.* Ed. Kent Gerard and Gert Hekma. New York: Harrington Park, 1989. 67–89.

Pommier Édouard. *Théories du Portrait: De la Renaissance aux Lumières.* Paris: Gallimard, 1998.

Rank, Otto. *Beyond Psychology.* New York: Dover, 1958.

– *The Double: A Psychoanalytic Study by Otto Rank.* Trans. and ed. Harry Tucker. New York: Meridian, 1971.

Rico, Francisco. 'Introduccion.' *El Caballero de Olmedo* by Lope de Vega y Carpio. Ed. Francisco Rico Madrid: Cátedra, 1981. 13–93.

Rodríguez, Evangelina, and Antonio Tordera. 'Introduccion biografica y crítica.' *Entremeses, jácaras y mojigangas.* Ed. Evangelina Rodríguez and Antonio Tordera, 9–81. Madrid: Castalia, 1982.

– *La técnica del actor español en el Barroco: Hipóptesis y documentos.* Madrid: Castalia, 1998.

Rodríguez Villa, Antonio. *La corte y monarquía de España en los años de 1636 y 37.* Madrid: Luis Navarro, 1886.

Rossi, Rosa. *Escuchar a Cervantes: Un ensayo biográfico.* Valladolid: Ambito Ediciones, 1998.

Ruggiero, Guido. *The Boundaries of Eros: Sex Crimes and Sexuality in Renaissance Venice.* New York: Oxford UP, 1985.

Sáez Raposo, Francisco. 'La herencia de la *Commedia dell'Arte* italiana en la conformación del personaje de Juan Rana.' *Bulletin of the Comediantes* 56.1 (2004): 77–96.

Saint-Saëns, Alain. 'Homoerotic Suffering, Pleasure, and Desire in Early Modern Europe, 1450–1750.' *Lesbianism and Homosexuality in Early Modern Spain: Literature and Theater in Context.* Ed. María José Delgado and Alain Saint-Saëns. New Orleans, LA: UP of the South, 2000. 3–86.

Sanders, Barry. *Laughter as Subversive History.* Boston: Beacon, 1995.

Serralta, Frédéric. 'Juan Rana Homosexual.' *Criticón* 50 (1990): 81–92.

Shapiro, Susan C. '"Yon Plummed Dandeprat": Male "Effeminacy" in English Satire and Criticism.' *Review of English Studies* n.s. 39 (1988): 400–12.

Smith, Bruce R. *Homosexual Desire in Shakespeare's England: A Cultural Poetics.* Chicago: U of Chicago P, 1991.

Stroud, Matthew D. 'Comedy, Foppery, Camp: Moreto's *El lindo Don Diego.*' *Lesbianism and Homosexuality in Early Modern Spain: Literature and Theater in Context.* Ed. María José Delgado and Alain Saint-Saëns. New Orleans, LA: UP of the South, 2000. 177–97.

Thompson, Peter. 'Crossing the Gendered "Clothes"-Line: Lanini y Sagredo's *El parto de Juan Rana.*' *Bulletin of the Comediantes* 53.2 (2001): 317–33.

- 'Fencing and Fornication in Calderón's *El desafío de Juan Rana*.' *Revista de estudios hispánicos* 37 (fall 2003): 497–507.
- 'Juan Rana, A Gay Golden Age *Gracioso*.' *A Society on Stage: Essays on Spanish Golden Drama*. Ed. Edward H. Friedman, H.J. Manzari, and Donald D. Miller. New Orleans, LA: UP of the South, 1998. 239–51.

Tomás y Valiente, Francisco. 'Delincuentes y pecadores.' *Sexo barroco y otras transgresiones premodernas*. Madrid: Alianza, 1990. 11–31.

Varey, J.E., and N.D. Shergold. *Teatros y comedias en Madrid: 1666–1687: Estudio y documentos*. London: Thames, 1974.

Velasco, Sherry. *Male Delivery: Reproduction, Effeminacy, and Pregnant Men in Early Modern Spain*. Forthcoming.

Vélez Quiñones, Harry. 'Deficient Masculinity: "Mi puta es el Maestre de Montesa."' *Journal of Spanish Cultural Studies* 1 (2001): 27–40.

Vega y Carpio. *Lope de El acero de Madrid*. Ed. Lazaro Montes de la Puente y Antonia Ayora. Madrid: Dirección General de *Ensenanza Media*, 1962.
- *El arte nuevo de hacer comedias en este tiempo*. Juana de José Prades. Madrid: Clásicos Hispánicos, Consejo Superior de investigaciones científicas, 1971.
- *El Caballero de Olmedo*. Ed. Francisco Rico. Madrid: Cátedra, 1994.

Webber, Andrew J. *The Dopplegänger: Double Visions in German Literature*. Oxford: Clarendon, 1996.

Weller Richmond, Celia E. *Spanish Literature: III. Towards a National Literature (11th Century to 15th Century): 'The Celestina.'* Microsoft ® Encarta ® Reference Library 2005. © 1993–2004 Microsoft Corporation.

Wilson, Edward M. Introduction. *Fieras afemina amor* by Pedro Calderón de la Barca. Kassel: Reichenberger, 1984. 1–54.

Index